STEAM Activities in 30 Minutes for
Elementary Learners

Purchases of AASL Publications fund advocacy, leadership, professional development, and standards initiatives for school librarians nationally.

❖

ALA Editions purchases fund advocacy, awareness, and accreditation programs for library professionals worldwide.

AASL Standards-Based Learning

STEAM Activities in 30 Minutes
for Elementary Learners

Deborah Rinio

CHICAGO | 2020

American Association of School Librarians

TRANSFORMING LEARNING

Deborah Rinio, PhD, is a former school librarian from Fairbanks, Alaska. She is currently an assistant teaching professor for the School Library Certification Program at Montana State University Bozeman and an adjunct instructor at the University of Alaska Fairbanks. She was a school librarian in elementary, middle, and high schools for the Fairbanks North Star Borough School District. She was on the AASL Standards and Guidelines Editorial Board that developed the *National School Library Standards*. She has served on various boards and committees including the ALA Policy Corps, Alaska Association of School Librarians, and Alaska Library Association. Her articles have been published in *VOYA, Knowledge Quest, School Library Connection,* and *School Libraries Worldwide.*

© 2020 by the American Library Association

Extensive effort has gone into ensuring the reliability of the information in this book; however, the publisher makes no warranty, express or implied, with respect to the material contained herein.

ISBN: 978-0-8389-4680-0 (paper)

Library of Congress Control Number: 2019054059

Composition by Alejandra Diaz in the Utopia Std and Galano Classic typefaces.

⊚ This paper meets the requirements of ANSI/NISO Z39.48-1992 (Permanence of Paper).

Printed in the United States of America

24 23 22 21 20   5 4 3 2 1

CONTENTS

PART III
Making STEAM Work for You

CHAPTER 5

CHAPTER 6

CHAPTER 7

ACKNOWLEDGMENTS

I am eternally grateful to my editors Jamie Santoro and Stephanie Book, who saw potential in this idea and encouraged its fruition. I would also like to thank Laura Connor, whose work with STEAM programs inspired the idea that became this book.

In addition to several school librarians who wished to remain anonymous, the following educators helped to test the activities in this book during the 2018–2019 school year with their learners. Their experience, guidance, and feedback were invaluable to this process.

Martha Tomeo, Tri-Valley School, Healy, Alaska
Rebecca Donald, Denali Elementary School, Fairbanks, Alaska
Kerry Brown, Kassun Elementary, Anchorage, Alaska

Finally, this book would not have been possible without the contribution of Christina Hum, who wrote the Technology Integration sections to accompany each activity. Christina, MEd Technology, is a science educator in Fairbanks, Alaska, and an educational technology maven. Her knowledge about and passion for a STEAM approach to education are inspiring.

INTRODUCTION

Using a STEAM Approach in the Classroom and the School Library

STEAM education is a transdisciplinary approach to the curriculum that enables learners to make authentic connections with the knowledge, skills, and processes of an art form along with another subject area in science, technology, engineering, or mathematics. Both artists and scientists engage in an iterative process of exploration, creation, and analysis. They both engage in observation, discussion, and refinement as they practice their profession.

The STEAM approach is applicable to any elementary classroom. Classroom educators can collaborate with music educators to explore the science of sound or the mathematics of musical rhythms and patterns; educators can partner with another classroom educator to engage learners in creating science journals of local flora and fauna. Inherent in these practices and in a STEAM approach is a focus on inquiry, collaboration, and learner-driven exploration, three of the six Shared Foundations in the *National School Library Standards for Learners, School Librarians, and School Libraries*, making STEAM a perfect approach for the elementary school library. Although any elementary educator can use this book for ideas and inspiration on how to approach STEAM education in their classroom, school librarians are the primary audience. The school librarian can be found at the intersection of inquiry and exploration in the school, supporting all subject areas and grade levels.

Furthermore, a scaffolded approach is used in each activity. The average elementary school librarian sees every learner in the school, often in blocks of thirty to forty-five minutes. The school librarian must shift from one class to another, often with only a few minutes between classes. School librarians may find themselves working with a class of kindergartners, immediately followed by a group of fifth graders, with no break before a class of second-grade learners. To accommodate such a schedule, which makes planning for hands-on activities difficult, the activities in this book were written so that the same activity, with the same (or very similar) materials, can be used either throughout the day with all learners or with one specific group of learners.

For example, in the activity "Coding with Cups: Designing a Structure Using Code," all learners use paper cups to build a structure and write a simple algorithm so that another group of learners can replicate the design using only the code. Kindergarten through second-grade learners write a simple arrow-based code, whereas third- and fourth-grade learners add the idea of replication in the design of their code, and fifth- and sixth-grade learners add the idea of loops to their code. Each set of learners engages in the same activity but at a greater level of complexity or cognition.

As learners engage in the inquiry and design processes, the path they follow may involve twists and turns. Inquiry is rarely linear, and true inquiry involves flexibility, allowing learners to determine the question or problem, the method for answering the question or solving the problem, and the ultimate conclusion or product. Given only thirty minutes, learners cannot engage in the full inquiry process, but they can be encouraged to engage in specific portions of the process, such as asking questions, using evidence to answer questions, sharing products, and reflecting on the process. Along the way, they will need to test and refine their ideas. In order to effectively engage in an iterative process, a growth mindset is needed.

Learners with a growth mindset will acknowledge "failures" as learning opportunities and necessary steps in the process, in contrast to learners with a fixed mindset who view failure as an identity. A person with a growth mindset might say, "The prototype failed," whereas a person with a fixed mindset might say, "I failed." This distinction becomes important because it has links to an individual's level of persistence, willingness to take risks, and likelihood of asking for help. For example, learners who have a fixed mindset might be afraid to ask for help because they perceive it as reinforcing their lack of intelligence or ability.

Fortunately, research shows that mindset can be shaped (Dweck, 2016; Good, Aronson, and Inzlicht, 2003; Smith, Brumskill, Johnson, and Zimmer, 2018). Chapter 2, "Applying a Growth Mindset," provides research and guidelines for fostering a growth mindset in our learners and ourselves. Additionally, growth mindset tips are provided within each activity. Encouraging learners to think of their skills and abilities as mutable not only is helpful in guiding them through the inquiry and design processes but also helps meet many of the Competencies in the Grow Domain within the *National School Library Standards*.

With the release of the *National School Library Standards for Learners, School Librarians, and School Libraries* (American Association of School Librarians [AASL] 2018), a need for lesson plans aligned to the new standards emerged. The six Shared Foundations of the *National School Library Standards*—Inquire, Include, Collaborate, Curate, Explore, and Engage—seem a natural fit for STEAM activities and lessons. True STEAM experiences involve the teaching of standards from at least two disciplines. In this book, the *National School Library Standards*, the Next Generation Science Standards, and the National Core Arts Standards are used as the basis for each activity. For educators seeking further STEAM or STEM collaboration opportunities, AASL also developed a *National School Library Standards* crosswalk with the Next Generation Science Standards, available through the AASL Standards web portal at standards.aasl.org.

HOW TO USE THIS BOOK

To set the stage for the activities, part I of the book focuses on the research and rationale behind a STEAM approach (chapter 1) and a discussion of how to apply a growth mindset (chapter 2).

Part II includes fourteen activities evenly divided into two sections: "Thinking Like a Scientist" (chapter 3) and "Designing Like an Engineer" (chapter 4). Each activity in this book is designed to be completed in a thirty-minute class period. The scientific principles addressed in these lessons are complex. In this short period, learners will not gain mastery in these concepts. Instead, view these activities as starting points or steps along the path toward understanding these topics; each activity is a starting point, not a destination.

Part III provides ideas and suggestions for educators who wish to write their own scaffolded lesson plans (chapter 5), collaborate with other educators in their school community (chapter 6), and assess learners' growth (chapter 7).

Activity Elements

The activities are divided into two categories: thinking like a scientist and designing like an engineer. The activities in the "thinking like a scientist" chapter rely primarily on the inquiry process. Learners are encouraged to ask questions, design and conduct experiments, and think critically about the world around them. The activities in the "designing like an engineer" chapter rely primarily on the exploration and design processes. Learners are encouraged to engage in iterative design and in trial and error testing and to think creatively.

Each activity includes the following components:

Essential Question. The essential question is a fundamental question used to guide the instruction across all grade levels. The question, like the standards, will not necessarily be answered fully over the course of the activity. However, it should be used as a guidepost for where the activity is going. If the activity is thought of as one piece of a larger unit, the essential question could be the goal for the unit as a whole.

Science Background for Educators. The "Science Background for Educators" section in each activity is intended to provide basic content for educators who are unfamiliar with the STEAM concepts in the activity. This content can also be shared with learners when developmentally appropriate and relevant to the curriculum.

National Standards. Each activity includes standards that align to the *National School Library Standards,* using the *AASL Standards Framework for Learners* (AASL 2018), the Next Generation Science Standards (National Research Council 2013), and the National Core Arts Standards (State Education Agencies Directors of Arts Education [SEADAE] 2015). Remember that each standard or competency is complex. No single standard is intended to be taught and mastered in a thirty-minute period. Learners need repeated exposure and practice for mastery.

Materials. Materials are designed to be inexpensive or easy to obtain through donations (e.g., empty plastic bottles, rubber bands, etc.). Quantities of each material needed are indicated, along with potential alternative materials where appropriate.

Scaffolded Exploration. Activities are scaffolded into three grade-level bands: kindergarten through second grade, third and fourth grades, and fifth and sixth grades. This particular breakdown is based on learners' developmental ability to engage in different types of activities. However, educators know their learners best. It is up to each educator to decide how to implement the activity and with what grade-level learner. For example, steps for kindergarten through second grade might be more appropriate for a particular group of third-grade learners, or the third- and fourth-grade activity might be something that second graders can easily obtain. Feel free to utilize activities in this way. Educators should make the activities work for them and their learners.

Assessment. Formative assessment ideas are provided for each activity to help ensure learner growth. Additional formative assessment ideas are available in chapter 7, "Assessing Learners' Work."

Technology Integration. Access to technology in school libraries and classrooms is variable, and young learners often require additional time because they need more instruction in the use of a specific tool. Therefore, the lesson plans in this book do not require technology. However, it is recognized that effective use of technology can offer learners the opportunity to examine authentic problems, complete more complex STEAM projects, and gain a better understanding of STEAM concepts.

The technology integration sections are designed to use technology in meaningful ways that extend STEAM and inquiry-based learning, as opposed to a substitution for textbook-style instruction. To that end, the technology integration exploration in each lesson plan is designed to be used in conjunction with the activity as a means of engaging learners with technology-based skills and applications while still meeting the content and skill goals of the activity. Each exploration integrates with the activity at a different stage (before, during, or after) as described in the exploration itself.

The technology integration exploration requires the use of Google Sheets, which is universally accessible and free to use. However, an educator could easily adapt the activities for use with Microsoft Excel or another spreadsheet software. Depending on computer availability and learner skill level, the technology integration exploration can be done as a whole-class, small-group, or independent activity. One technology integration idea is provided for each grade-level band within each activity. Educators should choose the one that works best for them and their learners or create their own.

An appendix toward the end of the book provides instructions for how to use each element of Google Sheets necessary to complete the technology integration explorations. At the end of the appendix is an Element Location Chart that indicates the activities in which each Google Sheet element is used.

Suggested Picture Books. The suggested picture books section in each activity can be used to provide context and background for the activity or as extensions to the activity. They are not intended to be read and discussed in the same thirty-minute period as the activity but should be done at a separate time. Of course, if time allows, they can certainly be used as a method of introducing learners to STEAM concepts before beginning the activity itself. The recommended age level is a starting point, but all books can be used with any group of learners. Conversation starters are included to help learners think critically and make connections between the concepts in the book and the activity.

References and Nonfiction Resources. References and nonfiction resources can be used to locate additional scientific background for educator and learner.

Remember that in addition to learning STEAM content knowledge, learners are developing skills in the six Shared Foundations of the *National School Library Standards* (AASL 2018). Giving learners the opportunity to practice Inquiry, Inclusion, Collaboration, Curation, Exploration, and Engagement in different content areas will help them improve their skills and see the value of these skills across content domains.

Whether you use every chapter of this book or just a few, the hope is that this book will inspire you to create opportunities to engage in STEAM practices, a growth mindset, and classroom educator and school librarian collaboration now and in the future.

PART I

Understanding STEAM and Its Role in the Elementary School Library

CHAPTER 1

Why STEAM?

STEM stands for Science, Technology, Engineering, and Mathematics and reflects a curriculum that puts special emphasis on inquiry-based learning. Learners engaging in a STEM curriculum are asked to solve problems and design solutions using STEM disciplines. In a STEAM approach to the curriculum, the arts are integrated into the STEM instruction. The arts are used to demonstrate understanding and construct meaning in the art form in question as well as a STEM subject area. Learners might use art to better understand STEM or use STEM to explore art.

With a STEAM approach, learning can take place through any artistic medium that uses creativity. Through this process, learners make authentic connections with the knowledge, skills, and processes of both the art form and another subject area. For example, in the activity "Making Dye: Examining Color," learners engage in the scientific method, learn about solutions, and practice the art form of dyeing fabric (in this case, thread). As a result of making the connections between the subject discipline and the art form, learners are able to make deeper connections to both sets of concepts.

Additionally, art provides a medium by which learners can visually and concretely process what might otherwise be abstract scientific knowledge. Young children (seven to eleven years of age) are still in the concrete operational stage of development (Inholder and Piaget 1958), which means that they depend on concrete mental operations and are unable to manipulate ideas mentally without the use of external tools such as illustrations, models, and manipulatives. For example, in the activity "Making a Tissue Box Guitar: Exploring Sound," learners use music to conceptualize pitch and wavelength by making a model in a way that makes an abstract concept more accessible for elementary-age learners.

A variety of skills used by both scientists and artists are not often taught explicitly in K–12 science instruction. These skills include the ability to draw on curiosity, to observe and then accurately express one's observations, to construct meaning from one's observations, to work effectively with others, to think spatially, and to think kinesthetically (Sousa and Pilecki 2012). These skills are common to both art and science and, thus, are more likely to be explicitly addressed in a STEAM approach to the curriculum.

THE VALUE OF THE ARTS

The arts, regardless of their position in the curriculum, play a natural role in the lives of young people. Much of what children do when they play is a natural form of art—singing, drawing, and dancing all engage the senses. These acts help create neural networks needed for successful learning. Visual-spatial areas of the brain are developed as children draw and finger paint. Singing and rhyming impact auditory, visual, and cognitive functions. Dancing and movement help develop gross motor skills. Music and color play roles in memory retention, such as learning the alphabet song or using different colors to remember the various states in the United States. Overall, these experiences contribute to emotional and academic well-being because learners are led to realize the different ways people express emotions and ideas (Sousa and Pilecki 2012).

The arts, like each component of STEM, are often thought of as separate subjects (visual arts, dance, music, etc.). Each art form has a discrete set of skills and knowledge that make it its own discipline. However, just like science, technology, engineering, and mathematics, the arts share a common set of cognitive behaviors. When taught explicitly, the arts can enable learners to develop knowledge, skills, and dispositions that help prepare them for college, career, and life.

In his article "What the Arts Do for the Young," Elliot Eisner (2002) laid out three reasons that art education should be prevalent in our nation's schools: shaping human form, creating meaning, and developing thinking. At the heart of his argument is the idea that the arts enrich the human experience. Art education helps learners to both experience and frame the senses into aesthetic forms, which produce emotional satisfaction. Although this type of satisfaction can be found in other experiences, such as observing the aurora or scoring a goal during a sports game, arts education asks learners to take note of these ideas and examine them in a conscious way—to learn how to observe them and also to create them. Not all learners will be able to express their ideas through art effectively, but being able to "read" the images and ideas in art enables us to use art to give voice to our feelings, "and with this voice the arts make forms of meaning possible that would otherwise remain mute" (p. 16).

Visualization is also an important concept in scientific thinking (Graham and Brouillette 2016). Scientists utilize models, diagrams, graphs, and visual images in the process of making discoveries. Learners may develop their observation skills by sketching in science notebooks or exploring a model of the water cycle to understand how water changes states. With guidance, even the youngest learners can create simple bar graphs to collect and analyze data—for example, a graph of birthdays by month. When learners create these sorts of visualizations, educators can use the results for formative assessment and identification of learners' misconceptions.

Studies examining arts integration have shown relationships between academic achievement and arts education (Hetland and Winner 2004), improvement in science and writing test scores (Catterall, Dumais, and Hampden-Thompson 2012), and increases in learners' long-term retention of content (Rinne, Gregory, Yarmolinskaya, and Hardiman 2011). For example, most of us are familiar with how music can help young learners remember information, such as learning the alphabet through song.

Similarly, in a study of nine, hour-long art–physical science lessons, Graham and Brouillette (2016) tested three models of education: (1) an educator in an isolated classroom using a STEAM approach, (2) a classroom educator and an art educator working in collaboration, and (3) a traditional classroom. The researchers found that learners performed better on science benchmarks when educators used model 1 or 2—in other words, when a STEAM approach was used.

CREATIVITY AND CRITICAL THINKING

One of the components of art that we naturally think of is creativity. In reality, creativity is a complex idea that is often hard to quantify and is not relegated to the arts alone. One study compared the brains of professional jazz pianists as they played memorized music and improvised music. When the pianists were playing extemporaneously, the areas of the brain associated with individuality and self-expression were more active, and the areas of the brain associated with inhibition and self-regulation were less active. The more creative the musician, the less inhibited and focused that musician was (Limb and Braun 2008). In other words, by letting go of their inhibitions, the musicians were able to be more creative.

The arts promote this sort of creativity through the development of both subtle and complex forms of thinking by asking learners to make judgments in the absence of a rule, to evaluate and express opinions on an idea that has no right or wrong answer. This type of thinking is often undervalued in our schools, and yet life is filled with these sorts of situations, such as deciding which house to purchase or writing a review of a product. Both of these examples involve making decisions based not only on logic but also on personal opinion in the absence of a specific rule. You aren't wrong just because someone doesn't like your house or agree with your movie review. However, traditional schoolwork often focuses learners on right or wrong answers instead of answers that are multifaceted and complex.

It's helpful to consider the two main types of thinking that people engage in when solving problems: convergent and divergent. Both types of thinking are present in STEAM fields. In convergent thinking, there is a piecing together of various bits of information to arrive at a single correct answer to a problem. Learners engage in convergent thinking when they are testing or calculating with defined outcomes. For example, a learner might be asked to find the wavelength of a particular frequency, test which of three different materials will produce the strongest bridge (with all other factors being the same), or calculate the density of an object after measuring its mass and volume.

In contrast, divergent thinking involves breaking a problem down into its component parts to investigate all possibilities and emerge with a solution. For example, in the activity "Building a Flashlight: Looking at Circuits," learners are asked to build a flashlight using common household items. Although there are multiple ways to approach the problem that will not produce light, there is no single, correct solution to this problem.

Both types of thinking are valid and necessary and will be engaged in during authentic inquiry. The engineer who uses convergent thinking to determine the strongest material for a bridge will use divergent thinking to produce several different designs that appeal to the aesthetic and usage demands of the community in which the bridge will be placed.

Jauk, Benedek, and Neubauer (2012) demonstrated greater brain wave activity associated with divergent thinking than with convergent thinking. This finding suggests that divergent tasks are more challenging, causing the brain to make new connections between neural networks, which increases creativity and improves one's ability to engage with complex and challenging problems (Takeuchi et al., 2010).

Schools, however, often focus primarily on convergent thinking. Standardized tests, for example, require a single, correct answer to a problem; yet, to foster critical thinking in learners, educators must provide experience with creativity and originality, which involves divergent thinking. In most U.S. schools, science curriculum is focused on carrying out experiments and solving problems for which the outcome is already known. Learners are not given opportunities to collect evidence, ask questions, or seek out possible answers (Sousa and Pilecki 2012).

Further, although activities that ask learners to engage in divergent, critical, or creative thinking are beneficial to the development of their skills, abilities, and dispositions, it is not uncommon for both learners and educators to be unfamiliar with this type of activity, or fail to recognize that it will require more time or effort than they are willing to expend. Yet studies show that learners demonstrate information-processing and creative-thinking skills at a much greater extent in inquiry-driven classrooms as opposed to traditional (textbook-centered) classrooms, as well as demonstrating a more positive attitude toward science classes and science educators (Yager 2007).

SHARED COMPETENCIES

In addition to a basic understanding of how the arts and sciences can be melded in inquiry-driven instruction, it is useful to examine the standards of each component part of the lesson and to see how they are similar or different. The competencies of art education often parallel the Shared Foundations of the *National School Library Standards* (AASL 2018), as well as the practices and crosscutting concepts in *A Framework for K–12 Science Education* that formed the basis of the Next Generation Science Standards (National Research Council 2012). Seeing how the various goals and concepts of these distinct units overlap can be useful in designing, implementing, or justifying STEAM lessons in your school library or classroom.

Shared Foundations

Six Shared Foundations and their Key Commitments form the backbone of the *National School Library Standards:*

- **Inquire:** Build new knowledge by inquiring, thinking critically, identifying problems, and developing strategies for solving problems.
- **Include:** Demonstrate an understanding of and commitment to inclusiveness and respect for diversity in the learning community.
- **Collaborate:** Work effectively with others to broaden perspectives and work toward common goals.
- **Curate:** Make meaning for oneself and others by collecting, organizing, and sharing resources of personal relevance.
- **Explore:** Discover and innovate in a growth mindset developed through experience and reflection.
- **Engage:** Demonstrate safe, legal, and ethical creating and sharing of knowledge products independently while engaging in a community of practice and an interconnected world.

Science and Engineering Practices

A Framework for K–12 Science Education served as the blueprint for the Next Generation Science Standards (NGSS). The document identified eight practices of science and engineering that reflect the inquiry and discourse practices that learners must engage in alongside content knowledge in order to fully understand scientific and engineering ideas.

1. **Asking Questions (for Science) and Defining Problems (for Engineering):** Learners should be able to ask questions about their readings, observations, and conclusions. They should be able to define problems and seek out information necessary to determine constraints and parameters of working toward a solution.

2. **Developing and Using Models:** Modeling includes the creation of diagrams, replicas, mathematical representations, and computer simulations. Models represent a system or parts of a system and thereby enable learners to ask questions, suggest explanations, make predictions, and communicate ideas.

3. **Planning and Carrying Out Investigations:** Investigations are used to describe a phenomenon, test a theory or model, or compare varying solutions to an engineering problem. Learners engaged in an explanation will identify the goal of the investigation, make predictions, collect data, and use data to support conclusions.

4. **Analyzing and Interpreting Data:** Once data are collected, learners must know how to present those data in a form that will reveal relationships and patterns, and effectively communicate results to others.

5. **Using Mathematics and Computational Thinking:** Mathematics is used to represent physical variables and their relationships. Learners might use computers or digital tools to observe, measure, record, and process data.

6. **Constructing Explanations (for Science) and Designing Solutions (for Engineering):** The goal of science is to construct explanations for various phenomena, while the goal of engineering is to solve problems. Learners will use models they have created or data they have collected to effectively make a claim or design a solution.

7. **Engaging in Argument from Evidence:** Argument is a necessary part of science and engineering, as it enables the best explanation for a phenomenon or the best design for a problem to emerge. Learners must use argumentation to compare and evaluate solutions.

8. **Obtaining, Evaluating, and Communicating Information:** Being able to read, interpret, and produce scientific and technical writing is fundamental to science. Learners must be critical of the information they read and communicate their own ideas effectively.

The Eight Competencies of Arts Education

In 2002, Elliot Eisner of Stanford University identified eight competencies of arts education. Sousa and Pilecki (2012) reenvisioned these eight competencies through the lens of a STEAM-focused curriculum. Further exploration reveals how the AASL Standards and the NGSS Science and Engineering Practices often parallel these competencies in practice (table 1.1).

1. **The perception of relationships.** When learners create a work of art in music, words, or another discipline, it helps them to see how pieces come together to form a whole. In the sciences, this skill enables a researcher to see how one part of an ecosystem affects other parts of the system (NGSS Practice: Analyzing and Interpreting Data). In information literacy, this competency often results in knowledge that forms the basis for new meaning and sparks curiosity (AASL Shared Foundation: Explore).

2. **An attention to nuance.** A learner who wishes to excel in the arts will learn that small differences can make a large impact in the final product. For example, a learner creating a visual representation (painting, sculpture, etc.) must make decisions about form, color, and style that will impact the work. In writing, this competency applies to the use of language needed for metaphor, allusion, innuendo, and the like (NGSS Practice: Obtaining, Evaluating, and Communicating Information). An engineer designing a bridge, for example, may need to take these same ideas into consideration to ensure that the bridge not only is structurally sound but meets the aesthetic needs of the community (AASL Shared Foundations: Inquire and Explore).

3. **The perspective that problems can have multiple solutions and questions can have multiple answers.** Unfortunately, schools too often focus learning on finding a single right answer. In reality, almost anything can be approached in multiple ways. In science, and in life, difficult problems require the exploration of multiple options from varying perspectives. There is rarely one right answer to a given problem (NGSS Practice: Constructing Explanations and Designing Solutions). Instead, individuals must realize the positive and negative consequences of their actions. A food scientist, for example, may be exploring how to reduce pest impact on crops; each option from pesticide use to genetic modification of the crops has positive and negative consequences that must be considered. To explore multiple solutions and explanations, a learner must also interact with diverse opinions and contribute to discussions in which multiple viewpoints on a topic are expressed (AASL Shared Foundations: Inquire and Include).

4. **The ability to shift goals in process.** Schools often oversimplify the process of discovery, which is not always linear. Although learners should be able to design and carry out a plan of inquiry, the process itself is often murky and unknown because new knowledge and curiosity can shift learners' paths and guide them down new avenues of investigation (AASL Shared Foundations: Inquire and Explore). A scientist who begins an experiment, only to encounter surprising results, may end up shifting the investigation to new avenues (NGSS Practice: Planning and Carrying Out Investigations). For example, the microwave oven was invented by accident when Percy Spencer, while testing a new vacuum tube for a radar project, discovered that a chocolate bar in his pocket melted faster than he expected. His curiosity was piqued. He began to experiment with the vacuum tube, and, after extensive investigation, the microwave oven was born.

5. **The permission to make decisions in the absence of a rule.** Although there are times and places for specific rules and processes, there are often times when individuals must use their best judgment to determine if something has been done well, is complete, or meets the specified requirements. This sort of judgment occurs in science when scientists "defend their explanations, formulate evidence based on a solid foundation of data, examine their own understanding in light of the evidence and comments offered by others, and collaborate with peers

in searching for the best explanation for the phenomenon being investigated" (National Research Council 2012, 52; NGSS Practice: Engaging in Argument from Evidence). In the inquiry process, learners make judgment calls when they use reflection to guide informed decisions and iteratively respond to challenges (AASL Shared Foundations: Include and Collaborate).

6. **The use of imagination as the source of content.** In the arts, imagination is critical to the process because an artist will use imagination to visualize situations and then make the best decision for the task at hand. In inquiry and the sciences, this sort of imagination fuels the curiosity that results in questions that ultimately lead to sustained inquiry (NGSS Practice: Asking Questions and Defining Problems; AASL Shared Foundations: Inquire and Explore).

7. **The acceptance of operating within constraints.** Within the arts, an individual is often constrained by a specific medium, such as paint, clay, sound, or movement. Artists work to use the constraints of their medium to invent new ways of interacting with content. Similarly, scientists develop and use models to explore understandings. Within the models and simulations they create, scientists can explore a variety of concepts and test hypotheses (NGSS Practice: Developing and Using Models). Whether used in art or science, or another discipline altogether, the inquiry process requires that learners question and assess the validity and accuracy of information (AASL Shared Foundations: Explore and Engage). These operating constraints—in art, science, and inquiry—can be seen as hindrances but also as opportunities to engage in creativity and investigate the possibilities offered within the given constraint.

8. **The ability to see the world from an aesthetic perspective.** Experience in the arts can help learners to see the world in new ways, such as the poetic nature of music, or the design of a building. Although the sciences do not help people see the world from an aesthetic perspective, they do encourage the use of scientific thinking in the form of analyzing and interpreting data, which involves identifying the significant features and patterns of the data (NGSS Practice: Using Mathematics and Computational Thinking). Similarly, learners engaged in inquiry will "[adopt] a discerning stance toward points of view and opinions expressed" (AASL 2018, Learner II.A.2.), enabling them to look at the world in new ways (AASL Shared Foundation: Include).

In addition to the eight competencies of art education (Eisner 2002), connections can be drawn to the National Core Arts Anchor Standards (SEADAE 2015):

- **Creating:** Conceiving and developing new artistic ideas and work.
  - Anchor Standard 1. Generate and conceptualize artistic ideas and work.
  - Anchor Standard 2. Organize and develop artistic ideas and work.
  - Anchor Standard 3. Refine and complete artistic work.

TABLE 1.1

Alignment of Eisner's competencies of art education, NGSS Science and Engineering Practices, and AASL Shared Foundations

Competencies of Art Education	NGSS Science and Engineering Practices	AASL Shared Foundations
The perception of relationships	Analyzing and Interpreting Data	Explore
An attention to nuance	Obtaining, Evaluating, and Communicating Information	Inquire, Explore
The perspective that problems can have multiple solutions and questions can have multiple answers	Constructing Explanations (for Science) and Designing Solutions (for Engineering)	Inquire, Include
The ability to shift goals in process	Planning and Carrying Out Investigations	Inquire, Explore
The permission to make decisions in the absence of a rule	Engaging in Argument from Evidence	Include, Collaborate
The use of imagination as the source of content	Asking Questions (for Science) and Defining Problems (for Engineering)	Inquire, Explore
The acceptance of operating within constraints	Developing and Using Models	Explore, Engage
The ability to see the world from an aesthetic perspective	Using Mathematics and Computational Thinking	Include

- **Performing, Presenting, Producing**

  Performing (dance, music, theatre): Realizing artistic ideas and work through interpretation and presentation.

  Presenting (visual arts): Interpreting and sharing artistic work.

  Producing (media arts): Realizing and presenting artistic ideas and work.
    – Anchor Standard 4. Select, analyze, and interpret artistic work for presentation.
    – Anchor Standard 5. Develop and refine artistic techniques and work for presentation.
    – Anchor Standard 6. Convey meaning through the presentation of artistic work.

- **Responding:** Understanding and evaluating how the arts convey meaning.
    – Anchor Standard 7. Perceive and analyze artistic work.
    – Anchor Standard 8. Interpret intent and meaning in artistic work.
    – Anchor Standard 9. Apply criteria to evaluate artistic work.

- **Connecting:** Relating artistic ideas and work with personal meaning and external context.
  - Anchor Standard 10. Synthesize and relate knowledge and personal experiences to make art.
  - Anchor Standard 11. Relate artistic ideas and works with societal, cultural, and historical context to deepen understanding.

As learners engage in well-designed STEAM activities, they will create, perform, produce, present, respond, or connect to art through the exploration of science, mathematics, and technology. For example, learners who design a bridge in an engineering challenge activity have the opportunity to connect to the artistic nature of the design in several ways. They can *create* an artistic idea in the design of the bridge. They might also *present* their bridge and share it with others. They might *respond* to the design of bridges as they study the form and *connect* the artistic nature of the bridge to historical bridge designs.

No matter what form the integration of art and STEM takes, learners who engage in an inquiry-driven model of instruction employ divergent, critical, or creative thinking that is beneficial to the development of their skills, abilities, and dispositions and that fosters a more positive attitude toward science. Utilizing a STEAM approach enables learners to creatively and concretely express scientific concepts through an artistic medium in a way that addresses science, art, and school library standards. When STEAM is used in the school library, learners interact with each other and with science content to think, create, share, and grow every day.

CHAPTER 2

Applying a Growth Mindset

The inquiry process can be challenging. It is not a linear path; there are often twists and turns as learners encounter new information, make predictions, engage in research, and communicate information. To engage effectively in the inquiry process requires a learner to be curious, persistent, tenacious, and willing to view failure as a learning opportunity. Unfortunately, many learners view their mistakes and failures as personal failings and challenges as a reflection that they are not smart. Fortunately, educators can help their learners develop a growth mindset. Having a growth mindset helps learners to see mistakes as opportunities to try again, challenges as opportunities for growth, and setbacks as pauses toward future success.

Dweck (2016) proposed two basic mindsets along a continuum: a fixed mindset and a growth mindset. People who trend toward a fixed mindset believe that their basic abilities, including intelligence and talents, are predetermined traits that cannot be altered. Those who trend toward a growth mindset believe that their abilities can be enhanced through learning and practice. They recognize that although there are limits to each person's capabilities, everyone can develop further and improve their abilities. A growth mindset is oriented toward learning and, therefore, promotes perseverance, resilience, and challenge seeking.

Learners with fixed mindsets who get a C on a test may think they just don't get it, can't do the work, or are just plain not smart. On the other hand, learners with growth mindsets who get a C on the exam will realize there is something more to learn, a new approach to be taken—in other words, they can improve their grade.

Dweck's (2016) research showed that people with a fixed mindset fear challenges and devalue effort, putting a greater emphasis on the immediate state of affairs.

GROWTH MINDSET CONTINUUM

Those with a growth mindset exhibit perseverance and resilience in the face of challenges, qualities that enable them to transform their current setbacks into future successes. In fact, learners with a fixed mindset will likely be afraid of exposing their deficiencies and, therefore, will turn down learning opportunities such as tutoring, denying themselves the opportunity to learn.

Mindsets also affect people's interest in the type of feedback that is presented to them. Those with a fixed mindset are only interested in feedback that reflects on their abilities. One study (Dweck 2016) showed that fixed mindset learners were only interested in which answers were correct or incorrect and had no interest in learning why an answer was correct or incorrect. Those with a growth mindset, on the other hand, valued learning itself, paying close attention to the information that would allow them to increase their knowledge.

It's worth noting that these two mindsets reflect a thought pattern that applies to all aspects of a person's being, not just intelligence. People hold beliefs about their artistic talent, sports ability, business acumen, and even personality. Those with a growth mindset see all those traits as mutable and able to be improved, while those with a fixed mindset believe them to be stable and unchanging. Of course, each individual can fall on a continuum between growth and fixed (figure 2.1) and may hold a fixed mindset regarding one aspect of their lives and a growth mindset regarding another. For example, a person might believe that her musical talent is mutable and can be improved but that her intelligence cannot. This person has a growth mindset when it comes to music and a fixed mindset when it comes to intelligence. Although technically there are not just two mindsets but a variety of possible mindsets along the scale between growth and fixed, for simplicity's sake Dweck (2016) contrasted the two, and the same technique is used in this book.

THE VALUE OF A GROWTH MINDSET FOR INQUIRY AND DESIGN

Holding a growth mindset can be a boon within the inquiry and design processes. The inquiry process involves a certain amount of ambiguity. When learners are engaged in asking and answering questions of personal or curricular significance to which there is no single answer, the path they follow may involve unknown twists and turns. Although educators provide guidance about the process of inquiry, they allow learners the flexibility to determine the question or problem, the method for answering the problem, and the ultimate conclusion or product. These unknowns mean that the process may not be linear or identical. As learners learn more, their questions may change; as they begin to answer one question, they may find themselves with new questions to ask. Depending on how they wish to communicate their results, they may need to acquire additional knowledge or skills. Having a growth mindset enables a learner to navigate this path with a greater degree of confidence.

Similarly, the design process involves testing and refining in an iterative way that includes both failure and improvement. During problem solving, engineers consider failure in various ways. The iterative nature of the design process itself presumes that aspects of a design are unlikely to be the best solution to the problem, that a particular prototype may be considered a failure if it does not produce the desired criteria.

In order to effectively engage in both the inquiry and design processes, individuals need a growth mindset. An individual with a growth mindset will acknowledge "failures" as learning opportunities and necessary steps in the process. This is in contrast to people who view failure as an identity rather than an occurrence. Those with a growth mindset will say, "The prototype failed" or "The product is a failure," whereas those with a fixed mindset will say, "I am a failure" or "I failed." As Dweck (2016) explained,

> In one world, failure is about having a setback. Getting a bad grade. Losing a tournament. Getting fired. Getting rejected. It means you're not smart or talented. In the other world, failure is about growing. Not reaching for the things you value. It means you're not fulfilling your potential. (p. 15)

To reach their fullest potential and engage openly in the inquiry and design processes, learners need a growth mindset. Luckily, mindsets are beliefs, which means they can be changed, and educators can help guide learners toward a growth mindset in the way they approach learning and the feedback they provide to learners.

In an analysis of a mathematics classroom, learners who were engaged in an inquiry pedagogy used ambiguity as a pathway to deepen their mathematical understanding (O'Brien, Fielding-Wells, Makar, and Hillman 2015). For example, in one classroom the educator asked her learners to create a cylindrical, liter-sized bottle when they had never been taught how to find the area of a circle. Although learners were initially confused, the educator probed and questioned them, prompting them to think of past experiences until they suggested a solution, stretching them so that the unknown became an opportunity for growth rather than frustration. Having a growth mindset enables learners to persevere through these types of challenges and learn more as a result.

This isn't to say that failure becomes something to strive for or that failure doesn't hurt. However, when people believe that they can improve themselves, they realize that failures don't define them and that failure isn't the end of the journey; paths to success still exist.

FOSTERING A GROWTH MINDSET

Most researchers believe that humans are born with a growth mindset. The source of this belief can be seen in the way that toddlers explore their world by playing with the things around them to make sense of those things. Young, school-age children will typically share this sense of play, curiosity, and eagerness to learn. Yet, by the end of elementary school, the attitudes and beliefs of learners often shift toward a fixed mindset as they internalize the overt and subtle language of the adults around them (Dweck 2016).

Although schoolchildren may have a temperament that causes them to lean toward one mindset or another, research shows that mindset can be shaped (Dweck 2016; Good et al., 2003; Smith et al., 2018). Praising intelligence leads learners to believe that intelligence is a fixed trait and thereby puts them in a fixed mindset. On the other hand, praising the process of learning encourages a growth mindset. A learner with a fixed mindset, regardless of skill level, will be reluctant to try challenging activities because of a fear of failure.

A learner's mindset is important to individual growth, but so too is the mindset of the educator. Educators who hold a fixed mindset believe that their learners have fixed abilities and that, therefore, as educators they have no influence on their learners' intellectual ability. Such educators may find themselves labeling learners. For example, Dweck (2016) described an educator who didn't believe that girls could do math. Although Dweck had been very successful at math in high school, her teacher's thinking shook the confidence she held in her abilities. In short, an educator's mindset can have a negative effect on a learner's mindset and, by extension, that learner's academic progress. Of course, educators do not set out to undermine their learners, but what they perceive as helpful judgment can send the wrong message.

Fortunately, research demonstrates that everyone can change their mindset and that educators can play a role in helping learners develop a growth mindset.

Offering Thoughtful Praise

Dweck (2016) and Sousa and Tomlinson (2011) offered a variety of suggestions for fostering a growth mindset in the classroom. One approach involves the type of praise that is used with learners. People—especially children—enjoy praise, particularly praise that focuses on intelligence or talent. That praise is welcome and boosting in the moment, but when the recipients experience a challenge, their confidence decreases. Educators who wish to help their learners develop perseverance can focus their praise on the effort that was expended rather than on the talent of the learner. Instead of saying, "You're smart!," a growth-minded educator might say, "You worked really hard!"

Understanding the Brain

Dweck (2016) cited several basic strategies that educators can use to encourage a growth mindset in their learners. In addition to shifting the way they offer praise and encouragement, educators can take time to teach learners how the brain changes with learning and how abilities are mutable and can be improved. Teaching learners about how the brain changes with learning involves explaining basic brain functions and how neurons in the brain form new connections when learners stretch themselves to learn something new. Learners who understand this basic concept recognize that working hard on something is part of the process of getting smarter, whereas learners with a fixed mindset will see struggle as a sign of deficiency, that they aren't smart enough to accomplish the task.

Using Real-World Examples

Educators can also offer examples of real people who were passionate about their subject and achieved success through hard work and persistence, as opposed to presenting only the invention, award, discovery, or the like that was the result of the hard work. By seeing the process that great scientists, mathematicians, engineers, artists, and others go through to become successful, learners can better appreciate the necessity for overcoming adversity, bouncing back after failures, and facing challenges head on.

Providing Meaningful Feedback

Another strategy involves making sure learners know that the educator is there to help them and that everyone can master new content with time, help, and their own individual effort. Dweck (2016) suggested that educators give feedback that focuses on the process rather than the product of learners' work. Rather than providing right or wrong evaluations of learners' work, educators should focus on the progress learners have made.

Dweck (2016) also advised educators to offer constructive criticism to learners that focuses on where they are and what they need to do to improve. Avoiding criticism in an effort to make learners feel good doesn't help them move forward. She suggested the use of the word *yet* as a stratagem: "You haven't mastered this yet," "You haven't learned this strategy yet," and so on. In this way, educators can shift from verbiage that cues learners to feel they are not good at something and instead indicate that learners are on the road toward but have not yet arrived at their destination.

If learners are protected from honest and constructive feedback, they will begin to experience advice, coaching, and feedback as negative rather than as helpful. Instead of recognizing what they can do to improve, their self-confidence will suffer. Although some people believe that discussion of failure may be too complex or disturbing for elementary learners, other educators point out that elementary learners are perfectly capable of engaging in a multistep, iterative design process that involves testing, redesign, and retesting (Lottero-Perdue and Parry 2017). Further, with effective modeling and prompting by educators, evaluation of failed designs promotes a growth mindset and leads learners to a greater understanding of the design process and the scientific principles at play in the design.

Encouraging Purposeful Dialogue

Educators can also foster learners' growth and STEAM content knowledge through engaging in purposeful dialogue. Instead of answering learners' questions, educators can guide learners to their own answers by asking questions that help them develop new ideas and make connections between existing knowledge.

For example, imagine learners who are exploring density. In one scenario, the learners follow a scripted set of steps. They pour one liquid on top of another, note the results, and make a conclusion. Now imagine another scenario: the learners pour oil into a glass of water. As they begin to observe and question, perhaps they wonder what other fluids might float on water. Instead of answering the question, the educator might ask, "How could we test that?," thereby encouraging the learners to think scientifically. As they continue to respond to purposeful questioning, the learners will design an experiment that can then be conducted in the classroom. Through this sort of exploration, as opposed to a scripted experiment, learners will make connections that will cement their learning while helping them to develop a growth mindset.

Additionally, the educator might remind the learners of previously completed activities or experiments that might help them make new connections, such as a density experiment in which an egg is floated in salt water. In this case, the educator might ask, "How is the oil floating on water similar to the egg floating in salt water?" As the learners make observations, the educator might also repeat what the learners are saying to clarify their ideas and demonstrate more precise scientific language.

Even such questions as "What do you think will happen?" or "What do you think is happening?" as different phenomena are observed can help learners go from simply having a sense of awe or excitement to experiencing scientific understanding. When educators guide learners by asking the right questions rather than delivering the answers, they allow a genuine process of inquiry to occur so that learners are generating their own investigations and hypotheses. This sort of structure also allows learners to make mistakes in a supported environment, which can help them gain confidence scientifically, artistically, and in all areas of life.

INTEGRATING A GROWTH MINDSET INTO EDUCATION

It's important to recognize that a growth mindset cannot be taught in isolation during a specific portion of the day; rather, it is reflected in everything that educators and learners do throughout the day. These strategies—offering thoughtful praise, understanding the brain, using real-world examples, providing meaningful feedback, and encouraging purposeful dialogue—should be integrated throughout the curriculum and across content areas. They are not relegated to the school library alone, to just STEAM content, or to a certain part of the day; instead they are pedagogical approaches that apply to any curricular area.

Successful educators set high standards for their learners—not just the ones who are already achieving but all learners. Successful educators introduce concepts and ideas that are challenging. Yet they also establish a culture of learning, caring, and support. They do this by teaching their learners to love learning, to think for themselves, and to work hard, and it all starts with a growth mindset for themselves and their learners.

PART II

STEAM Activities

CHAPTER 3

Thinking Like a Scientist

A STEAM approach to any curriculum, incorporating the Next Generation Science Standards, involves science, engineering, and technology. Each discipline shares commonalities but is also distinct, just as dance, singing, visual arts, and theater each has its own practices and conventions even though the National Core Arts Standards are inclusive of all artistic forms. Yet, all disciplines, including STEAM disciplines, share common practices that overlap with the *National School Library Standards*.

The Next Generation Science Standards outline eight science and engineering practices (National Research Council 2012). These practices represent what learners are expected to do. The practices occur separately, but in a full inquiry unit they would also overlap and flow from one to another. For example, "asking questions" may lead to "planning and carrying out an investigation" that, in turn, would lead to "analyzing and interpreting data," all of which would fall within the Inquire Shared Foundation of the *National School Library Standards*.

Learners engage in these practices regardless of whether they are involved in a scientific, engineering, or technological pursuit. However, the form each practice takes will be different in each of these disciplines, just as it would in a social studies classroom.

The seven activities in this chapter focus on the skills a learner would employ to think like a scientist. Learners who think like a scientist will study how nature works. They will perform experiments using the scientific method (figure 3.1) to form testable explanations of observable phenomena. In doing so, they might ask questions and analyze data (Inquire), evaluate scientific information (Engage), design and conduct experiments individually (Explore) and collaboratively (Collaborate), engage in scientific debate (Include), seek a variety of sources (Curate), and communicate results (Inquire and Engage).

FIGURE 3.1

SCIENTIFIC METHOD

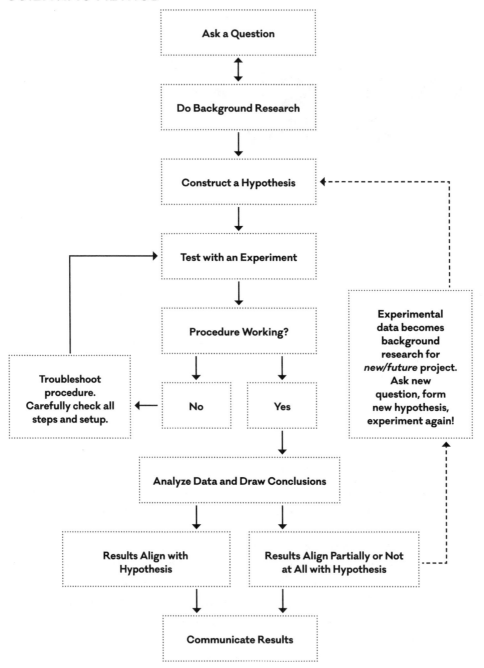

IMAGINING
EXPLORING SCIENTISTS

In this activity, learners will be asked to envision what a scientist looks like by drawing a picture. After comparing their results, learners will look at photographs of some scientists and discuss how the photos are the same as and different from the pictures the learners drew. A short discussion about who can be a scientist (anyone!) and what attributes scientists have in common (a growth mindset) will conclude the activity. Scaffolding will consist of the complexity of critical-thinking questions and discussion strategies.

Essential Questions
- What does a scientist look like?
- Who can be a scientist?

Science Background for Educators

Since 1983, the Draw-a-Scientist Test (DAST) has been used to examine learners' and educators' perceptions of scientists. Over the years, studies using the DAST have revealed stereotypes and misconceptions that learners and educators hold regarding what scientists look like and do. The original DAST results featured a man in a lab coat surrounded by beakers and books. Over time, however, this stereotypical image has shifted. As more women have entered scientific fields, more learners are drawing women in their DAST drawings. However, as they grow older, children tend to associate science with men more frequently, and their drawings depict scientists as primarily white.

★ COLLABORATION TIP

If there is a local university or science-based industry in the area, the school librarian may wish to invite a local scientist to visit the school library or a classroom. Learners can also talk to real scientists in the school library or classroom through services such as Skype a Scientist. Either way, learners should generate questions for the scientist before the conversation. After studying scientists over the course of the quarter, semester, or year, learners can repeat this activity and compare their two drawings. Do they imagine scientists differently now? Why or why not?

National Standards

Grade Level	AASL Standards Framework for Learners	Next Generation Science Standards: Science and Engineering Practices	National Core Arts Anchor Standards
K–2	I.A.1. Learners display curiosity and initiative by formulating questions about a personal interest or a curricular topic. I.A.2. Learners display curiosity and initiative by recalling prior and background knowledge as context for new meaning. III.B.1. Learners participate in personal, social, and intellectual networks by using a variety of communication tools and resources. III.B.2. Learners participate in personal, social, and intellectual networks by establishing connections with other learners to build on their own prior knowledge and create new knowledge.	**Practice 4. Analyzing and Interpreting Data** • Use and share pictures, drawings, and/or writings of observations. • Compare predictions (based on prior experiences) to what occurred (observable events). **Practice 7. Engaging in Argument from Evidence** • Distinguish between explanations that account for all gathered evidence and those that do not. **Practice 8. Obtaining, Evaluating, and Communicating Information** • Describe how specific images (e.g., a diagram showing how a machine works) support a scientific or engineering idea.	Anchor Standard 1. Generate and conceptualize artistic ideas and work. Anchor Standard 6. Convey meaning through the presentation of artistic work. Anchor Standard 10. Synthesize and relate knowledge and personal experiences to make art.
3–4 **5–6**	I.C.1. Learners adapt, communicate, and exchange learning products with others in a cycle that includes interacting with content presented by others. V.D.2. Learners develop through experience and reflection by recognizing capabilities and skills that can be developed, improved, and expanded.	**Practice 4. Analyzing and Interpreting Data** • Compare and contrast data collected by different groups in order to discuss similarities and differences in their findings. **Practice 8. Obtaining, Evaluating, and Communicating Information** • Read and comprehend grade-appropriate complex texts and/or other reliable media to summarize and obtain scientific and technical ideas and describe how they are supported by evidence.	

Materials

- White paper
- Crayons, colored pencils, markers

Activity

 THINK

1. Ask learners to imagine a scientist at work. What does the scientist look like? What is the scientist wearing? Where is the scientist working? What sort of equipment or tools does the scientist have to help in scientific work?
2. Other than providing these basic instructions, do not influence what learners will draw by giving them suggestions or examples.

 CREATE AND SHARE

3. Distribute paper and ask learners to draw the scene they just imagined. Ask them to be as detailed as they can.
4. Ask learners to use three descriptive words to complete the sentence "My scientist is _____." As needed, help learners write their words on their paper.
5. Ask learners to share their scientist drawing with a partner. Have them explain what kind of scientist they drew, what the scientist is doing, where the person is working, and the three words they used to describe their scientist.
6. As a class, or in groups, have learners compare their drawings. What is similar? What is different? As learners share, make a list of the different types of scientists they were able to name.

 GROW

7. Show learners pictures of some real scientists who reflect a variety of cultures and genders from books or from "This Is What a Scientist Looks Like" available at http://lookslikescience.tumblr.com/.
8. Ask learners what characteristics they need to become more like a scientist. Make a list on the board.
9. If time allows, ask learners to think about what type of scientist they would like to be and why and then draw a second picture. This time they should draw themselves doing science.
10. Ask learners what they can do to develop the skills necessary to become a scientist (e.g., practice doing science, realize that scientists fail often and keep trying, be more observant, be curious, etc.).
11. Before closing the activity, share with learners that any of them can be a scientist if they want. Scientists work in many different places and in many different ways, from astronauts and engineers to zoologists and biologists to environmental scientists and meteorologists.

★ GROWTH MINDSET TIP

Use the analogy of an iceberg with learners when discussing success. The part of the iceberg you can see above the water is success, but there's a lot under the surface that you never see: failure, hard work, disappointment, dedication, goals, and persistence.

Assessment

Collect learners' drawings. If learners did two drawings, how did the drawings change? Do learners' drawings reflect their understanding of what scientists do and that they too can be scientists?

Technology Integration

Learners will generate a radar graph to show what they think are the characteristics of a scientist compared to pictures and characteristics of real scientists.

Before Exploration

1. Create a Google Sheet and add the following column headings: "What do you think a scientist looks like?" "What does a scientist look like?" "What do you think a scientist does?" "What does a scientist do?" (See "Create a New Sheet" in the appendix.)
2. *Optional*: Create a form with the same four questions shown in item 1 (see "Creating a Form" in the appendix).

Exploration

Kindergarten through Second Grade

During the Create and Share activity, while learners are drawing, move around the room and collect two or three words from each learner that reflect what that learner thinks a scientist is. Place these words in column A or enter them into the form. When done, generate a radar chart (see "Radar Chart" in the appendix). Ask learners what everyone's responses have in common and what they do not have in common. Ask learners why. Show several different pictures of scientists during the Grow portion of the activity and ask learners to write or type words describing what they see into column B. Create another radar chart. Compare the two charts. Ask learners to describe the characteristics of a scientist.

Third and Fourth Grades

During step 4 of the activity, learners write down three words that describe a scientist. Ask them to type these words into column C of the Google Sheet. Select the data and create a radar chart (see "Radar Chart" in the appendix). Ask learners what their responses have in common and what is different.

In step 7 of the activity, learners will look at pictures of actual scientists. In step 8 of the activity, learners will generate a list of characteristics they need to become scientists. Type their responses into column D. What does the class think is the most important trait?

Create a new radar chart with the data from column D. Ask learners to compare the two radar charts.

Fifth and Sixth Grades

Share the Google Sheet with learners or link to the Google Form. Instead of completing step 4 of the activity, direct learners to interview five other learners using the questions in each heading of the Google Sheet. Learners should enter one-word answers in each cell or on each question of the form. Guide learners to generate a radar chart (see "Radar Chart" in the appendix). Share a class Google Sheet and ask learners to copy and paste their data into the shared sheet to generate a class list. Generate a class radar chart. As a class, compare the charts.

At the conclusion of the activity, ask learners if having additional information changes their ideas about the traits a person needs to be a scientist. As an optional activity, learners can copy and paste the words into a Google Doc, use a word cloud generator such as Wordle (http://www.wordle.net/) to make a word cloud of each set of data, and then compare the two lists in word cloud form.

Suggested Picture Books

These suggested picture books are designed to expose learners to the breadth of individuals who have, and can, become scientists. Books depict men and women of varying ethnicities and backgrounds from the past to today who have made contributions to science and engineering.

....

Title: *Marvelous Mattie:*
How Margaret E. Knight Became an Inventor
Author: Emily Arnold McCully
Suggested Grade Levels: K–6

Summary: The life of Margaret E. Knight is depicted in this book—how she was interested in machines as a girl, invented a paper bag folding machine, won a battle in court over her right to patent her invention, and became a successful inventor.

Conversation Starters:
1. What is a prototype, and why did Mattie need one?
2. What event got Mattie interested in inventing? What did she invent?
3. What steps did Mattie take to invent her paper bag folding machine?

Title: *Summer Birds: The Butterflies of Maria Merian*
Author: Margarita Engle
Suggested Grade Levels: K–3

Summary: In the middle ages, people called butterflies *summer birds* because they appeared in the summer. Everyone thought the summer birds were born from the mud and were evil—everyone, that is, except thirteen-year-old Maria Merian, who captured a butterfly in a jar and watched its life cycle from egg to caterpillar to butterfly.

Conversation Starters:
1. Why did people think butterflies came from mud?
2. How did Maria discover how butterflies are born?
3. What else did Maria observe?

Title: *Mae Among the Stars*
Author: Roda Ahmed
Suggested Grade Levels: K–2

Summary: This is the story of Mae Jemison, the first African American woman in space.

Conversation Starters:
1. Why do you think the educator suggested that Mae should be a nurse?
2. How did Mae achieve her dream?
3. What did Mae's mom and dad tell her to remember?

Title: *Whoosh! Lonnie Johnson's Super-Soaking Stream of Inventions*
Author: Chris Barton
Suggested Grade Levels: 2–5

Summary: Meet the inventor of the Super Soaker, one of the most popular toys of all time.

Conversation Starters:

1. What challenges did Lonnie face as a young inventor?
2. How did Lonnie contribute to NASA?
3. What inspired Lonnie to make the Super Soaker?
4. What does it mean to persevere? How did Lonnie persevere when no one wanted to buy his invention?

REFERENCES AND NONFICTION RESOURCES

Chambers, D. W. 1983. "Stereotypic Images of the Scientist: The Draw-a-Scientist Test." *Science Education* 67 (2): 255–65.

Losh, S. C., R. Wilke, and M. Pop. 2008. "Some Methodological Issues with 'Draw a Scientist Tests' among Young Children." *International Journal of Science Education* 30 (6): 773–92.

Miller, D. I., K. M. Nolla, A. H. Eagly, and D. H. Uttal. 2018. "The Development of Children's Gender-Science Stereotypes: A Meta-Analysis of Five Decades of U.S. Draw-a-Scientist Studies." *Child Development* 89 (6).

MAKING A TISSUE BOX GUITAR
EXPLORING SOUND

This lesson incorporates science and art with inquiry-based learning. Learners explore the ideas of pitch and sound as they make music with rubber bands and empty tissue boxes. In kindergarten through second grade, learners explore sounds as a class. In third and fourth grades, learners are challenged to find the rubber bands that produce the highest and lowest frequency pitches. In fifth and sixth grades, they apply the ideas of frequency and pitch to create a guitar-like instrument.

Essential Questions
- How does frequency impact pitch?
- How can experimentation be used to solve a problem?

Science Background for Educators
Sounds are made by vibrations. These sound vibrations travel through the air to our ears (figure 3.2). The vibration of the air causes the eardrum to vibrate, which, in turn, causes the bones in the middle ear to vibrate. The vibrating bones then cause a fluid in the inner ear to vibrate, which activates a nerve that carries a signal to the brain. The brain tells us we've heard a sound.

FIGURE 3.2

ILLUSTRATION OF SOUND VIBRATIONS AND THE EAR

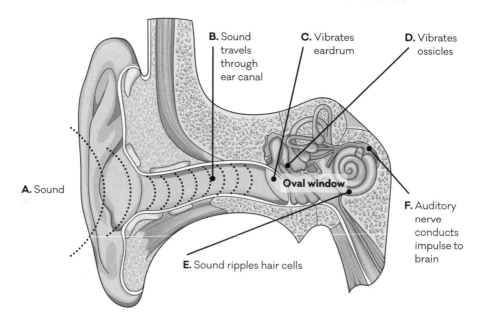

B. Sound travels through ear canal

C. Vibrates eardrum

D. Vibrates ossicles

A. Sound

Oval window

E. Sound ripples hair cells

F. Auditory nerve conducts impulse to brain

The speed at which an object vibrates creates the pitch of the sound. The slower the vibration, the lower the pitch, like that of a tuba; the faster the vibration, the higher the pitch, like that of a piccolo. The measurement that describes the speed of a vibration is called the *frequency,* which refers to how many times something moves back and forth in one second (figure 3.3). Humans have the ability to hear sounds at frequencies between twenty times per second and twenty thousand times per second. Dogs have a wider range; they can hear sounds with frequencies between fifteen times per second and fifty thousand times per second.

When learners begin to explore their rubber bands, they will notice that the thinner rubber bands make a higher pitch than the thicker rubber bands. The same concept applies to stringed instruments: a thicker guitar string will vibrate more slowly than a thinner one of the same length. This result occurs because heavier things are harder to move and, therefore, given the same push or energy, a lighter object will move faster than a heavier one.

Tension also plays a role in sound. The more tension on a string, the faster it will vibrate, meaning that it has a greater frequency and higher pitch. On a stringed instrument, such as a violin or guitar, the musician will adjust the tension on a string to give it the right pitch by turning the tuning peg for that string. A string can also be made shorter by pressing it against the fingerboard. This action produces a note with a higher pitch.

FIGURE 3.3

FREQUENCY WAVELENGTH DIAGRAM

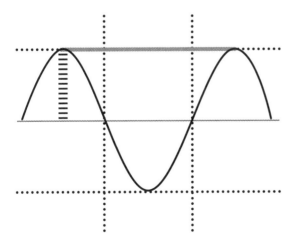

Wavelength (λ)
Distance between identical points on consecutive waves

Amplitude
Distance between origin and crest (or trough)

Frequency (ν)
Number of waves that pass a point per unit time

Speed
= wavelength x frequency

COLLABORATION TIP

After helping learners explore sound in the school library, the school librarian can collaborate with the music or classroom educator to continue the investigation. Learners can continue to explore pitch and frequency by examining the upper and lower ranges of various musical instruments.

National Standards

Grade Level	AASL Standards Framework for Learners	Next Generation Science Standards: Science and Engineering Practices	National Core Arts Anchor Standards
K–2	I.B.1. Learners engage with new knowledge by following a process that includes using evidence to investigate questions. I.D.3. Learners participate in an ongoing inquiry-based process by enacting new understanding through real-world connections. V.A.3. Learners develop and satisfy personal curiosity by engaging in inquiry-based processes for personal growth. V.C.1. Learners engage with the learning community by expressing curiosity about a topic of personal interest or curricular relevance.	Practice 3. Planning and Carrying Out Investigations • Plan and conduct an investigation collaboratively to produce data to serve as the basis for evidence to answer a question.	Anchor Standard 2. Organize and develop artistic ideas and work.

Grade Level	AASL Standards Framework for Learners	Next Generation Science Standards: Science and Engineering Practices	National Core Arts Anchor Standards
3–4	I.A.2. Learners display curiosity and initiative by recalling prior and background knowledge as context for new meaning. I.B.1. Learners engage with new knowledge by following a process that includes using evidence to investigate questions. III.A.2. Learners identify collaborative opportunities by developing new understandings through engagement in a learning group. III.D.1. Learners actively participate with others in learning situations by actively contributing to group discussions. V.C.1. Learners engage with the learning community by expressing curiosity about a topic of personal interest or curricular relevance.	**Practice 2. Developing and Using Models** • Use a model to test cause and effect relationships or interactions concerning the functioning of a natural or designed system.	Anchor Standard 2. Organize and develop artistic ideas and work.
5–6	I.A.2. Learners display curiosity and initiative by recalling prior and background knowledge as context for new meaning. I.B.3. Learners engage with new knowledge by following a process that includes generating products that illustrate learning. III.A.2. Learners identify collaborative opportunities by developing new understandings through engagement in a learning group. V.B.1. Learners construct new knowledge by problem solving through cycles of design, implementation, and reflection. V.C.3. Learners engage with the learning community by collaboratively identifying innovative solutions to a challenge or problem. V.D.1. Learners develop through experience and reflection by iteratively responding to challenges.	**Practice 5. Using Mathematics and Computational Thinking** • Use mathematical representations to describe and/or support scientific conclusions and design solutions.	

Materials

- Rubber bands of varying thicknesses and sizes (at least five different types)
- Empty tissue boxes (1 per learner or 1 per group)
- Scissors
- *Optional*: Stringed instrument such as a violin or guitar

Activity

 THINK

1. Explain that together, the class will explore sound.
2. Show learners an empty tissue box with a rubber band around it (figure 3.4). Pluck the rubber band to demonstrate how it makes a sound.

FIGURE 3.4

RUBBER BAND AROUND EMPTY TISSUE BOX

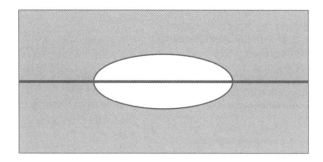

3. Have kindergarten through second-grade learners take turns plucking the rubber band. As a group, discuss what they hear. What questions do learners have about the sound?
4. For third- through sixth-grade learners, point out that the rubber band is moving up and down to create a wave and the speed at which it vibrates impacts the sound. Ask the class, "If sound is produced by a wave, what does it mean when there is silence?" (Hint: No sound waves are being produced.) Right at the end of the vibration, when it stops, there is silence.
5. Ask third- through sixth-grade learners to form small groups. Give each group a tissue box and two rubber bands (one skinny and one fat). Ask learners to put both rubber bands on their box and pluck each one. How are the sounds different?
6. With third- through sixth-grade learners, introduce the terms *pitch* and *vibration*. Explain that when learners plucked the thinner rubber band, it made a

high-pitched sound. The higher the pitch, the faster the vibration, so the thinner rubber band must have vibrated faster than the thicker rubber band. The thicker rubber band produces a lower pitch; therefore, it vibrated slower. Explain that this principle applies to stringed instruments, too. If you have access to a guitar or violin, show learners that each string has a different thickness. The thicker strings make lower sounding pitches than the thinner strings.

7. Give third- through sixth-grade learners two new rubber bands of the same thickness but different lengths. Ask learners to remove the rubber bands already on the box and put the new rubber bands on the box so that one is looser fitting around the box than the other. How do these rubber bands sound different?

8. For third- through sixth-grade learners, introduce the word *tension* and point out that the smaller rubber band has more tension on it than the larger rubber band; the smaller one is stretched out more around the box and has less flexibility. Learners should notice that the rubber band with more tension has a higher pitch. Once again, show learners the stringed instrument and point out how the musician will tighten the strings with the tuning pegs to make the pitch go up or down. Demonstrate this idea by tuning one string up and then back down.

9. Show fifth- and sixth-grade learners a diagram of a wave (see the "Science Background for Educators" section and figure 3.3). Introduce or reinforce the terms *wavelength* and *frequency*. Explain that the velocity (or speed) of the vibration is measured by multiplying the wavelength times the frequency. This calculation determines how fast the wave is traveling and the corresponding pitch of the sound. Ask learners which string on the instrument would have the greatest velocity (is vibrating the fastest).

 CREATE

10. Form small groups of kindergarten through second-grade learners and give each group an empty box and a mix of rubber bands. Ask learners to put a rubber band on their box and pluck it. Allow learners to explore on their own with the different rubber bands for a few minutes. What do they discover? Have them try the following experiments, recording the results on chart paper for the whole class:

    a. Try stretching the rubber band farther away from the box. Is the resulting sound different?

    b. Add a second rubber band that is skinnier or fatter than the first. What happens now?

    c. Try a longer and a shorter rubber band so that one has more tension on it than the other. How does that sound?

11. As you discuss these concepts with kindergarten through second-grade learners, introduce the term *vibrate* or *vibration*. Point out that the rubber band is vibrating to produce the sound.

12. Ask third- and fourth-grade learners to explore independently the different sounds they can make with the tissue box and rubber bands. Which rubber band makes the highest pitched sound? Which makes the lowest? Which is vibrating fastest? Which has the most tension on it? Provide a log on which learners can record their observations, or help them create one (see Worksheet 3.1: Sound Log Worksheet).

13. For fifth- and sixth-grade learners, explain that their challenge for the time remaining is to create a rubber band guitar with five "strings." Learners should put the rubber bands on the box in order of size so that each one increases in pitch. Learners may need to use scissors to cut the opening of the box wider to accommodate five rubber bands.

> ★ **GROWTH MINDSET TIP**
> If learners struggle with the activity and begin to show their frustration, encourage them to change their words. Instead of saying, "I give up!" encourage them to say, "I can keep trying!" or "My first plan didn't work, but I will try another strategy."

 SHARE

14. As a class, briefly review what learners found in their investigations. Were learners able to answer any of these questions? Are there new questions? What questions do third- and fourth-grade learners have about pitch, vibration, and tension?

 GROW

15. If time and materials allow, provide each learner with a box and have all learners sit together in a circle. Practice making music by trying different rhythms and rubber band configurations.

16. Ask fifth- and sixth-grade learners to label their "strings" 1 through 5 before trying to play a song. Can they play "Mary Had a Little Lamb"? Can they write their own song using the "string" numbers? As a class, discuss what worked, what didn't, and how they tried different approaches to solve the problem.

Assessment

Ask kindergarten through second-grade learners what the rubber band is doing when it moves back and forth (vibrating). Have third- and fourth-grade learners write their answers and questions from step 14 on an exit ticket. As fifth- and sixth-grade learners engage in the Create portion of the activity, circulate around the groups and check for understanding by asking why they are making certain decisions. Were they successful at making a "guitar"?

WORKSHEET 3.1

SOUND LOG

Fill out the chart to record your observations.

Rubber Bands	Pitch	Vibration
Skinny		
Fat		
Short		
Long		

Which rubber band makes the highest pitched sound?

_____

_____

Which rubber band makes the lowest pitched sound?

_____

_____

Which rubber band vibrates fastest?

_____

_____

Which rubber band has the most tension on it?

_____

_____

Technology Integration

Learners will collect and graph data to represent sound waves, amplitude, and frequency.

Before Exploration

1. Create a Google Sheet (see "Create a New Sheet" in the appendix) and add a second sheet (see "Adding Sheets" in the appendix).

2. On Sheet1, title columns A, B, and C as "Object," "Sound," and "Vibrate," respectively. Title column E as "Rubber Band Type" and column F as "Sound." Fill column A with objects you have available, such as tissue box, plastic bottle, and the like. Fill column E with the rubber band types: thick, thin, long, and short. Fill columns B and C with checklists (see "Insert a Checkbox" in the appendix). *Optional*: Add pictures of rubber bands and objects instead of words to columns A and E by using Insert > Image from the Google Sheet menu (see "Insert an Image" in the appendix).

3. On Sheet2, title columns A and B as "Time" and "Placement of Rubber Band," respectively. Under column A, number each cell 1 through 5. Skip column C. Title column D as "Placement of Thin Rubber Band" (0 to 4 centimeters and 0 to -4 centimeters) and column E as "Amplitude" (scale: 1 = low, 3 = high). Copy and paste columns D and E into columns F and G and relabel for the thick rubber band.

4. On the tissue boxes, mark a scale 1, 2, 3, and 4 centimeters from the hole on one side and -1, -2, -3, and -4 centimeters on the other side of the hole perpendicular to where the rubber band is plucked, with 1 and -1 starting closest to the hole on either side. The center line will be 0 (figure 3.5).

FIGURE 3.5

TISSUE BOX WITH RUBBER BAND AND SCALE LABELING

Exploration

Kindergarten through Second Grade

Prior to completing the activity, ask learners to explore which objects make sound using rubber bands and other provided objects, checking the boxes in columns B and C. Ask learners what the results show about objects that make sounds. Ask if there is an easier way to view this information. Demonstrate how to select columns A and B and create a bar graph with aggregated data (see "Column Chart or Bar Chart" in the appendix).

Again, ask learners what this shows about objects that make sounds. Ask if there is an easier way to view this information. In step 3 of the activity, show learners how to place a thick and a thin rubber band on a tissue box and pluck the rubber band to see if it makes a high sound or a low sound. Ask learners to enter H (High) or L (Low) for each rubber band type in column F. Graph the data from columns E and F as an organizational chart (see "Organizational Chart" in the appendix). Ask learners if they see any patterns.

Third and Fourth Grades

After completing the activity, demonstrate how to place the thin rubber band on the box, then pull the rubber band back to a certain distance and release, listening to the resulting sound. Ask learners if the sound is loud or soft on a scale of 1 to 3 (1 = quiet, 3 = loud). Add their responses to column E. Select the data in columns C and D and graph as a line graph (see "Line Chart" in the appendix). Ask learners if they think the sound volume changed with greater distance from the middle of the box. Ask learners to repeat the process for the thick rubber band, placing data in columns F and G. Next, ask how learners could model the movement of the rubber band on a graph over time.

Explain that the rubber band's vibration motion from the top, through the center, to the bottom is a wave that can be graphed. Direct learners to pull the rubber band and estimate the height it reaches as it moves from the top through the center and down to the bottom. Tell learners to *estimate* (because the rubber band moves fast) and record the greatest distance the rubber band reaches as it oscillates back and forth past the center line 0, counting 1, 2, 3, and so on each time it hits the top, the middle, and the bottom (figure 3.6). Select columns A and B and graph as a line graph.

Fifth and Sixth Grades

Repeat the Exploration for third and fourth grades. If needed, refer to the "Science Background for Educators" section for definitions of *amplitude* and *wavelength*. Using the thick rubber band, show learners how the amplitude changes over time as the rubber band loses energy and the crests of the wave become smaller. Ask learners to

FIGURE 3.6

RUBBER BAND MOVING BACK AND FORTH

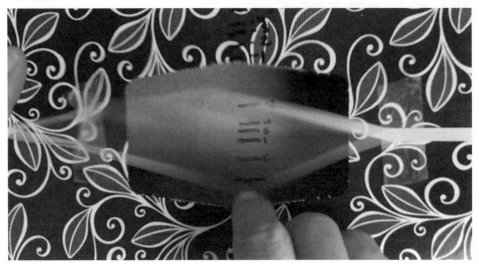

repeat this process for the thin rubber band. Ask learners if the amplitude is different for the thick and thin rubber bands. Learners should see that the frequency or wavelength distance is smaller for a thin rubber band, resulting in a change in pitch. Guide learners to the idea that this principle is the same on a guitar string or even in our voice box.

Extension

Use the Google Science Journal app to record the intensity (amplitude) and the pitch of sounds and have the app automatically graph the data. Ask learners to explain and discuss the graphs.

Suggested Picture Books

These suggested picture books address sound and how we hear and interpret sound in our daily lives. *Swish and Squeak's Noisy Day* depicts the typical noises a child hears at home and at school. In *The Sound of Silence,* a young boy sets out to hear silence. *The Sound of All Things* is about a boy who is asked to describe sounds to his deaf parents who can't hear them for themselves. In *What's That Sound?* a young boy is scared of the sounds he hears in his new home until his sister helps him see what each sound really is.

Title: *Swish and Squeak's Noisy Day*
Author: Birgitta Sif
Suggested Grade Levels: K–2

Summary: As Swish and Squeak go about their day, Swish hears a variety of sounds.

Conversation Starters:
1. Why does Swish think she hears an alligator chomping the kitchen table into tiny pieces?
2. When Swish says she hears an elephant trampling down the stairs, what is it really?
3. List all the sounds Swish hears throughout the day.

Title: *What's That Sound?*
Author: Mary Lawrence
Suggested Grade Levels: 1–3

Summary: When Tim's family moves to the country, he is scared by all the new sounds, but his sister helps him see that every sound can be explained.

Conversation Starters:
1. What was Tim scared of?
2. Why does Tim's dad think it's quiet? Why does Tim disagree?
3. What's the word for things that shake back and forth?

Title: *The Sound of Silence*
Author: Katrina Goldsaito
Suggested Grade Levels: K–4

Summary: While walking through Tokyo, Yoshio hears a variety of sounds. When a musician tells him that her favorite sound is *ma*, the Japanese word for "silence," he sets out to hear this sound himself.

Conversation Starters:
1. Compare the sounds Yoshio hears in Tokyo with the ones you hear in your town.
2. Define *onomatopoeia* (words that sound like what they describe). Common examples are *hoot, swish,* and *bark*. What words does Yoshio use to describe the sounds he hears?
3. Where did Yoshio find silence?

Title: *The Sound of All Things*
Author: Myron Uhlberg
Suggested Grade Levels: 1–5

Summary: A hearing boy and his deaf parents enjoy Coney Island, where the father asks his son to describe the sounds he hears all around them through sign language.

Conversation Starters:

1. How do you "feel" sound?
2. How did the boy find new words to describe the ocean to his father?
3. What words did the boy use to describe the fireworks? What other words could you use?

REFERENCES AND NONFICTION RESOURCES

Gardner, R. 2013. *Experimenting with Sound Science Projects*. Berkeley Heights, NJ: Enslow Publishers.

———. 2005. *Jazzy Science Projects with Sound and Music.* Berkeley Heights, NJ: Enslow Publishers.

MAKING DYE
EXAMINING COLOR

In this activity, learners will investigate water-based dyes made with a variety of plants and household items. Kindergarten through second-grade learners will work together as a class to guess which dye was produced by which material. Learners in third and fourth grades will test how the color changes based on time spent in the dye bath. Learners in fifth and sixth grades will work in groups and experiment with producing different shades of the same color. All groups will dye string and use it to make art.

Essential Questions
- How are dyes made?
- How does time affect the darkness of dye color?

Science Background for Educators

When we see different colors, we are seeing the light that is reflected off various surfaces. The wavelength of the light determines what color we see. Red is the longest wavelength (about 700 nanometers), violet is the shortest (about 400 nanometers), and all the other colors are in between.

Although human brains can distinguish about ten million different colors, each color we see is a mixture of three basic colors (red, green, and blue). When all three are mixed together, the result is white light. When none are present, black light results.

Paint and pigment work a little differently than light, because they are not light sources. They mix together differently than light does, so the three primary colors are not red, green, and blue but, rather, red, yellow, and blue. Additionally, when you mix all three primary colors together, you get the opposite of what occurs with light—instead of the colors combining to form white, they combine to form black. This happens because paints do not have a color of their own—the color you see is white light minus whatever color the paints absorb.

More than fifteen thousand years ago, our ancestors used colors to paint. These early colors were natural substances such as clay and stone that were crushed into pigments. Although we don't know the exact date, dyes from natural sources have been used to color textiles for at least six thousand years.

Pigments are easier to apply than dyes because the finely ground particles of pigments are suspended in a fluid and applied to the surface of the material. Dye, on the other hand, is a colorant that is completely dissolved in a liquid. To be applied, the dye must be absorbed by the fiber in question.

Unfortunately, dyes are more likely to fade. Additionally, some dyes and fabrics require a mordant (a substance that acts as a bond between the two materials) to be fixed more permanently to the fiber.

Dyeing is as much an art as a science because of the variability in the process. Most plants cannot be relied upon to produce the same color in the same way each time. Growing conditions, harvesting times, the freshness or dryness of the material, and the methods of extracting the color all impact the depth of color. Additionally, the fiber being dyed, the length of time in the dye bath, and the mordant used will impact the richness and hue of the color, as well as how long the color will last.

Another variable that will influence color is the quantity of material used. It is recommended that equal weights of dyestuff and fibers be used. For example, if you were going to dye two ounces of string with onion skins, you would want to use two ounces of onion skins. The more fiber added, the more diluted the color will be.

 COLLABORATION TIP

After learners explore dyes in the school library, classroom educators and school librarians can collaborate to build on this lesson by helping learners design their own experiments involving food- and plant-based dyes, based on questions generated during the assessment. Learners can also create more involved artistic pieces by dyeing cloth or using the dyed thread in other applications.

Materials
- Saucepan
- Water
- Sieve
- Heating element such as a stove or hot plate
- Fruit, vegetable, and plant matter (e.g., onion skins, tree leaves [birch and oak in particular], turmeric, beets, various berries, tea, red cabbage, etc.)
- Glass jars for storage and transport (1 jar per batch of dye)
- Plastic cups (4 per group)
- Pencil (or straw, stick, ruler, etc.)
- Wool or cotton yarn, white, cut into 12-inch lengths (4 lengths per group)
- *Optional*: Colored yarn

Preparation
Most plant materials will need to simmer for one hour to extract their color. As a result, you will need to make the dye outside class time or recruit a classroom educator with older learners to make the dyes. You will want to make at least four batches of dye, but you can make more if desired. If possible, spend some time one day demonstrating the various materials that will be used to make dyes. Ask learners to predict what

National Standards

Grade Level	AASL Standards Framework for Learners	Next Generation Science Standards: Science and Engineering Practices	National Core Arts Anchor Standards
K–2	I.A.1. Learners display curiosity and initiative by formulating questions about a personal interest or a curricular topic. I.B.1. Learners engage with new knowledge by following a process that includes using evidence to investigate questions.	**Practice 1. Asking Questions and Defining Problems** • Ask and/or identify questions that can be answered by an investigation.	Anchor Standard 1. Generate and conceptualize artistic ideas and work.
3–4	I.A.1. Learners display curiosity and initiative by formulating questions about a personal interest or a curricular topic. I.B.1. Learners engage with new knowledge by following a process that includes using evidence to investigate questions. V.A.2 Learners develop and satisfy personal curiosity by reflecting and questioning assumptions and possible misconceptions.	**Practice 1. Asking Questions and Defining Problems** • Ask questions that can be investigated and predict reasonable outcomes based on patterns such as cause and effect relationships.	
5–6	I.A.1. Learners display curiosity and initiative by formulating questions about a personal interest or a curricular topic. I.B.1. Learners engage with new knowledge by following a process that includes using evidence to investigate questions. V.A.2. Learners develop and satisfy personal curiosity by reflecting and questioning assumptions and possible misconceptions. V.C.3. Learners engage with the learning community by collaboratively identifying innovative solutions to a challenge or problem.	**Practice 1. Asking Questions and Defining Problems** • Ask questions that arise from careful observation of phenomena, models, or unexpected results, to clarify and/or seek additional information.	

color each of the different items will make and then show learners how the color is made using water, a saucepan, and a stove or hot plate. Then, during learners' next visit to the school library, complete the activities.

To make the dyes, put the dyestuff into a pan and cover with eight cups of water. Bring to a boil and then reduce to a simmer. Simmer for one hour. Strain the colored liquid through a sieve into a glass jar for storage and transport to the classroom.

Activity

 THINK

1. Show learners the different colors of dye and dyestuff used to make the dyes. Explain or demonstrate how the dyes were made.
2. Ask learners to guess which color came from which material and then reveal the answers.
3. Ask fifth- and sixth-grade learners how they could design an experiment to test how the color will change when materials are left in the water longer. As a class, design an experiment.

 CREATE

4. Form groups of learners and give each group four cups with dye (make sure cups are labeled with the food or material used in that dye). Also, provide each group of kindergarten through second-grade learners four strings, four pencils, four lengths of tape, and one empty cup. Provide third- and fourth-grade learners one empty cup, twelve strings, four pencils, and five lengths of masking tape (each about six inches long). Provide fifth- and sixth-grade learners the materials needed to conduct their experiment.
5. Ask kindergarten through second-grade learners to tape one string to each pencil and third- and fourth-grade learners to tape three strings onto each pencil (or do this for learners ahead of time to save class time) and set the pencils on top of the cups so the strings are dipped into the liquid.
6. Ask third- and fourth-grade learners to label the strings "5," "10," and "15" by writing on the tape in marker.
7. Guide fifth- and sixth-grade learners through the experiment as needed.
8. While the strings are soaking, hand out the Dye Time Log (Worksheet 3.2) to kindergarten through second-grade and third- and fourth-grade learners and have them record their predictions about what color the strings will be. After five minutes, have kindergarten through second-grade learners remove the strings and hang them over an empty cup, and then record the actual color on the Dye Time Log; third- and fourth-grade learners can remove the strings labeled 5, tape them to their worksheet, then repeat with string 10 at ten minutes and string 15 at fifteen minutes.

DYE TIME LOG

Tape a section of string in each box.

Dye Material	5 Minutes	10 Minutes	15 Minutes

SHARE

9. Ask learners to share their results. Were their predictions correct? What was surprising? Ask third- and fourth-grade and fifth- and sixth-grade learners how this type of investigation might be useful if they were going to dye strings or yarn for various crafts.

> **GROWTH MINDSET TIP**
>
> As learners start to make connections, recognize their successes with specific language, such as "I'm impressed with your creative thinking." If learners are frustrated with their results, remind them that science isn't always predictable and is often challenging, but with persistence they can master it.

 GROW

10. Discuss how some colors are lighter than others. Ask learners what they could try to get a darker color (soak in the dye longer, use more material in the initial making of the dye, heat the dye, etc.).

11. In the remaining class time, provide learners with index cards, pencils, glue, and string. If there isn't enough string from the activity, supplement with other colored yarn. Allow learners time to explore with the materials and see what sort of design they can make.

Assessment

Ask learners to complete an exit ticket listing the questions they still have about dyeing thread or making dye from food.

Technology Integration

Learners will use conditional formatting in Google Sheets to examine color to predict new colors, saturation, shades, and color patterns.

Before Exploration

1. Create a new Google Sheet (see "Create a New Sheet" in the appendix). Rename Sheet1 "K–2" and label columns A, B, and C, respectively, "Color 1," "Color 2," and "New Color" (figure 3.7).

2. In column A, rows 2–6, enter "red," "red," "blue," "blue," "yellow." Repeat for rows 7–14.

3. Set up conditional formatting to change column B and C cells to colors based on what is entered in column A (see "Conditional Formatting" in the appendix).

FIGURE 3.7

SCREEN SHOT OF GOOGLE SHEET

	A	B	C
1	Color 1	Color 2	New Color
2	red	y	o
3	red	b	p
4	blue	r	p
5	blue	y	g
6	yellow	r	o
7	yellow	b	g
8	red	white	light red
9	Red		dark red

4. In cells F1, G1, H1, and I1, enter the following headers, respectively: "Dye Material," "5 min," "10 min," and "15 min."
5. Enter "Dye 1" in cell F2, "Dye 2" in cell F3, and "Dye 3" in cell F4.
6. Add a grid with width and height to 60 below row 7 (see "Creating Grids" in the appendix).
7. Duplicate sheet K–2 and rename it "3–4" (see "Adding Sheets" in the appendix). Label cell G1 "5 min," cell H1 "10 min," and cell I1 "15 min."

Exploration

Kindergarten through Second Grade

Before or after completing the activity, ask learners to predict the color in column C if yellow is mixed with red. Type "y" for yellow in cell B2 to see the resulting color in cell C2. Have learners repeat this with rows 3–9.

Ask learners to explain what happens with rows 8 and 9 when white or black is added to red. Next, ask learners to imagine a pattern of colors that might result if a piece of white yarn were to be dyed by dipping it into a series of different colors. Write learners' responses in column E.

Third and Fourth Grades

Before conducting the activity, complete the kindergarten through second-grade Exploration.

After completing step 8 in the Create section of the activity, ask learners to record their color predictions on the Google Sheet by using the Insert Color button to shade the cells in columns G, H, and I.

After completing the activity, instruct learners to hold the colored string from the activity next to the screen to determine how accurate their predictions were. Ask learners why they think the colors in their cells are similar to or different from the dye colors on the string.

Fifth and Sixth Grades

Share the Google Sheet with learners so they can make a copy (see "Sharing Sheets" in the appendix). During step 4 in the Create portion of the activity, show learners the different dyes and ask them to predict what color their string will be when dipped in each dye for the same length of time. Show learners how to create conditional formatting so that the cell is colored to match the letter in the cell that represents a certain color (i.e., y = yellow; see "Conditional Formatting" in the appendix).

After the activity, ask learners to fill column A with letters to represent colors and column B with the fill color based on the conditional formatting. Challenge learners to use the Fill Color button (see "Fill Color" in the appendix) to create a pattern in columns C and D that they could replicate with dye if they were to dip their strings into two different colors of dye. For example, if B1 is red and C2 is yellow, D2 might be orange. Experiment with dye and string to test learners' predictions if time allows.

Suggested Picture Books

The suggested picture books are all about colors—how colors combine (*Color Dance*), how blind people see color (*The Black Book of Colors*), and how new colors were invented (*The Day-Glo Brothers*). Each book provides opportunities for learners to ask questions about the nature of color and how we use color in our daily lives.

....

Title: *Color Dance*
Author: Ann Jonas
Suggested Grade Levels: K–2

Summary: Three dancers demonstrate how colors combine to make new colors.

Conversation Starters:
1. What colors mix together to make orange? Green? Purple?
2. What are words for different shades of green? Different shades of orange? Different shades of red?
3. What happens when all the colors are mixed together?
4. What happens when white is added to the colors? Or when gray is added? Or black?

Title: *The Black Book of Colors*
Author: Menena Cottin and Rosana Faría
Suggested Grade Levels: K–3

Summary: Using raised black lines and poetic prose, the author and illustrator describe what it's like for a blind person to "see" colors.

Conversation Starters:

1. How would you describe various colors?
2. What do you think of when you think of red? Blue? Yellow? Orange? Green?
3. Can you feel or smell colors? Why would Thomas describe colors in this way?

Title: *The Day-Glo Brothers: The True Story of Bob and Joe Switzer's Bright Ideas and Brand-New Colors*
Author: Chris Barton
Suggested Grade Levels: 4–6

Summary: This is the story of Bob and Joe Switzer, who invented the bright oranges, yellows, and greens we see today.

Conversation Starters:

1. What are some things you've seen that use Day-Glo colors?
2. What was the brothers' initial motivation for experimenting with fluorescence?
3. How do the Day-Glo colors help make people safer?
4. Did the brothers achieve their life goals? Why or why not?

REFERENCES AND NONFICTION RESOURCES

Dean, J. 2010. *Wild Color: The Complete Guide to Making and Using Natural Dyes*. New York, NY: Watson-Guptill Publications.

Kenney, K. 2015. *The Science of Color: Investigating Light*. Minneapolis, MN: Abdo Publishing.

Nankivell-Aston, S., and D. Jackson. 2000. *Science Experiments with Color*. Danbury, CT: Franklin Watts.

MAKING A SPIDERWEB
INSECT EXPLORATION

After discussing how spiders make their webs, learners will build webs. Kindergarten through second-grade learners will build one giant web as a class and discuss the different shapes they see in the web. Third- and fourth-grade learners and fifth- and sixth-grade learners will work in groups to make a web using string tied to classroom chairs. Learners will then compare their spiderwebs to images of real spiderwebs.

Essential Questions
- What do spiderwebs look like?
- How are spiderwebs made?
- How do spiders use their webs?

Science Background for Educators

Inside a spider are six little sacs called *glands*. Inside these glands is a liquid called *dope*. Each gland holds a different kind of dope. As the spider draws the dope out of the spinnerets on the bottom of its abdomen, the dope turns into a threadlike substance composed of silk.

Spider silk is stronger than the same-sized steel thread. People want to take advantage of the strength of spider silk to make things, but spiders don't produce enough silk to make such use practical. Five thousand spiders would only produce enough silk to make one dress.

Different types of spiders make different types of webs, depending on the purpose of the web. Sticky webs are typically used for catching prey. Stretchy webs are used for making egg cases.

Each type of spider makes its web in a slightly different way. The orb weaver spider makes her web by bridging a gap between two stable surfaces, such as two sticks (figure 3.8). Once she's finished the frame of her web, she starts to build the inside like spokes on a wheel; each thread is connected to the others at the middle. Then she creates a spiral from the center to the outer edge. Until that point, her web has not been sticky. It is merely the frame of the web. Finally, the spider replaces the spiral she made with a sticky silk, eating the temporary spiral along the way.

Argiope (ar-JIE-oh-pee) spiders make ultraviolet webs that people can't see, but other insects can. These webs mimic the patterns that a bee or wasp sees on some flowers, luring the insect to the web. Each species of Argiope makes its own web patterns (figure 3.9), and some change patterns when they make a new web.

Golden orb weaver spiders can change the color of their webs based on the light; they spin gold webs in sunny places and white webs in shady places to make it harder for the insects to spot the web.

These are just a few types of spiders and the ways they use their webs. There are hundreds more!

★ **COLLABORATION TIP**

During the Think phase of the activity, learners generate lists of questions they have about spiders. After conducting this activity in the school library, the classroom educator could continue the inquiry process by allowing the class to research one of the questions posed. Over several days or weeks, the school librarian can help learners find information, document sources, and take notes while the classroom educator devotes time for learners to read and put together presentations or products. When their projects are finished, learners can display them in the school library.

FIGURE 3.8

BUILDING A WEB

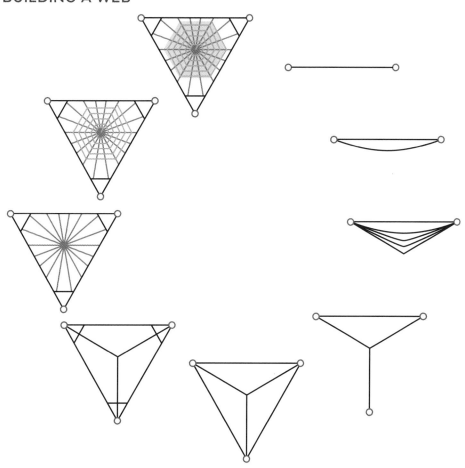

FIGURE 3.9

WEB IN A HONEYCOMB PATTERN

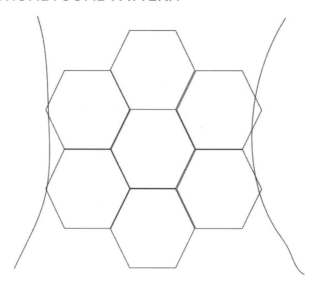

Materials

- Ball of yarn (1 per group)
- Scissors (1 pair per group)
- Small ball (e.g., cotton ball, pompom, ball of paper)

Activity

 THINK

1. Draw a spider on the board and ask learners what they already know about spiders. Ask them what questions they have about spiders.
2. Explain that today, learners will learn about spiderwebs and the different shapes they can have.

CREATE

3. Ask learners to sit in a circle on the floor. Explain that they will make one large web by rolling the ball of yarn from person to person. Roll the yarn to a learner and direct that learner to roll it to another person. After all learners have participated, ask them to hold their portion of the yarn tight and stand up.
4. Explain that different types of spiders make differently shaped webs but that all of them make their webs one thread at a time, like the learners did with their giant

National Standards

Grade Level	AASL Standards Framework for Learners	Next Generation Science Standards: Science and Engineering Practices	National Core Arts Anchor Standards
K–2	I.A.1. Learners display curiosity and initiative by formulating questions about a personal interest or a curricular topic. I.A.2. Learners display curiosity and initiative by recalling prior and background knowledge as context for new meaning. I.B.1. Learners engage with new knowledge by following a process that includes using evidence to investigate questions. IV.C.3. Learners exchange information resources within and beyond their learning community by joining with others to compare and contrast information derived from collaboratively constructed information sites. III.D.1. Learners actively participate with others in learning situations by actively contributing to group discussions.	Practice 8. Obtaining, Evaluating, and Communicating Information • Read grade-appropriate texts and/or use media to obtain scientific and/or technical information to determine patterns in and/or evidence about the natural and designed world(s). • Describe how specific images (e.g., a diagram showing how a machine works) support a scientific or engineering idea.	Anchor Standard 10. Synthesize and relate knowledge and personal experiences to make art.
3–4	I.A.1. Learners display curiosity and initiative by formulating questions about a personal interest or a curricular topic. I.A.2. Learners display curiosity and initiative by recalling prior and background knowledge as context for new meaning.	Practice 8. Obtaining, Evaluating, and Communicating Information • Obtain and combine information from books and/or other reliable media to explain phenomena or solutions to a design problem.	
5–6	V.B.1. Learners construct new knowledge by problem solving through cycles of design, implementation, and reflection. III.C.1. Learners work productively with others to solve problems by soliciting and responding to feedback from others. III.D.1. Learners actively participate with others in learning situations by actively contributing to group discussions.	Practice 8. Obtaining, Evaluating, and Communicating Information • Critically read scientific texts adapted for classroom use to determine the central ideas and/or obtain scientific and/or technical information to describe patterns in and/or evidence about the natural and designed world(s).	

web. Share some of the types of webs spiders make (see "Science Background for Educators").

5. Remind learners that a triangle has three sides. Toss a small object such as a cotton ball, pompon, or ball of paper into the web. Ask learners whether the shape the ball landed in is a triangle. Allow learners to take turns tossing the ball. To avoid ruining the web between throws, retrieve the ball and hand it to the next learner.

6. Explain that third- and fourth-grade and fifth- and sixth-grade learners will now make their own webs in groups using the legs of two chairs and some yarn. The legs of the chairs will form the outer frame of the web. Give learners about ten minutes to make the best web they can with their yarn. They may cut their yarn but should not use glue, tape, or the like.

  SHARE AND GROW

7. Allow third- and fourth-grade and fifth- and sixth-grade groups to examine each other's webs. Have learners describe how they made their web and explain what was easy and what was difficult. What did they learn from each other?

> ★ **GROWTH MINDSET TIP**
> Encourage learners to focus not on which web is "best" but on a positive feature of each web, such as creativity, neatness, accuracy, complexity, and so on.

8. Give learners an opportunity to look at images of spiderwebs from nonfiction books or an online gallery. Ask them to share what they learned about spiderwebs from the pictures, then compare their web to the ones the spiders created. What's the same? What's different?

9. If time allows, ask third- and fourth-grade and fifth- and sixth-grade learners to modify their webs or create a new web that is more similar to a spider's web and explain what changes they made and why.

Assessment

Do learners' responses in step 8 reflect an understanding that spiders make lots of different types of webs for different purposes?

Technology Integration

Learners will use Google Sheets to explore the process of spiderweb design using Lists to put the steps in order and help identify patterns. Older learners will explore the Fibonacci sequence created by the spiral pattern using Fill Color.

Before Exploration

1. Create a Google Sheet (see "Create a New Sheet" in the appendix) with two sheets (see "Adding Sheets" in the appendix).
2. In Sheet1, add the following headings to cells A1 through D1, respectively: "Step," "Description," "Shapes," and "Evidence."
3. In the column titled "Description," create a List with the following statements (see "Lists via Data Validation" in the appendix):
   a. Make spokes to outside circle
   b. Make spiral around
   c. Make outside circle
   d. Make inside circle
   e. Replace thread with sticky thread

4. Skip cell E1 and add the following headings to cells F1 through H1, respectively: "My Spiderweb," "Same," and "Real Spiderweb."
5. Insert an image of a spiderweb (See "Insert an Image" in the appendix).
6. On Sheet2, enter the following headings in cells A1 through C1, respectively: "Number," "Sequence," and "What Is the Pattern?"
7. On Sheet2, in cells A2 through A9, enter the numbers 0 through 7, respectively, in each cell. Enter "0" in cell B2 and "1" in cell B3. In cell B4 enter the equation "=B3+B2," and then drag to copy down through cell B9 (see "Copying and Pasting Text" in the appendix). See figure 3.10 for an example.
8. Replicate figure 3.11 by using the Fill Color button beginning with column J (see "Fill Color" in the appendix).

FIGURE 3.10

K-2 DATA SHEET

Number	Sequence	What Is the Pattern?
0	0	
1	1	
2	1	
3	2	
4	3	
5	5	
6	8	
7	13	

Exploration

Kindergarten through Second Grade

After the activity, show learners Sheet1 with the picture of the spiderweb, and ask them how they think the spiderweb was created. Show them the List of steps under the Description column and ask them to choose which one they think goes first, then second, and so on. When they are done, tell them the actual order in which a spiderweb is made, or show a video of a web being made.

Third and Fourth Grades

Repeat the instructions for the kindergarten through second-grade exploration, being sure to have learners describe the shapes created at each stage of the web creation process. Then ask learners to identify how the spiderweb they made during the activity compares to a real spiderweb by adding statements to columns F1, G1, and H1.

Fifth and Sixth Grades

After learners have completed the activity, ask them if there was anything in common between their spiderweb and a real spiderweb. Point out the spiral pattern created in an orb weaver spider's web. Next, show learners the list of numbers in Sheet2 and ask if they see a pattern in column B. Help learners to see that the pattern is the

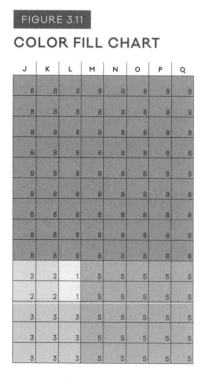

FIGURE 3.11

COLOR FILL CHART

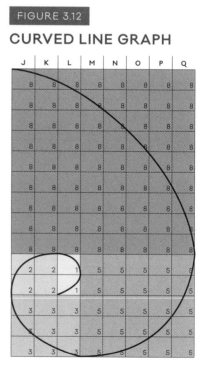

FIGURE 3.12

CURVED LINE GRAPH

current and preceding cells being added together. Explain that this process is known as the *Fibonacci sequence* and is the pattern responsible for the spiral patterns we see throughout nature, including spiderwebs.

Ask learners to graph the data with a simple line graph using the Explore button (see "Explore Button" in the appendix). Show learners how to draw a curved line from the line graph into the colored squares marked "1" (see figure 3.11). Ask learners what would happen if they repeated the curved line starting in each colored block from one corner to the other—for example, starting in the corner of the "2" box and arching around to the opposing box with a "2" (see figure 3.12). Ask learners if this pattern is similar to that of a spiderweb.

Suggested Picture Books

The featured books for this activity provide fictional examples of spiders making webs. Learners can read individual books to explore the reasons spiders might make webs, compare fiction to nonfiction, or do both. Throughout the pages of the book, *The Very Busy Spider* provides a realistic portrayal of a spider making a web by building the frame and then adding the spiral from the center to the outside. In *Sophie's Masterpiece,* Sophie the spider goes from room to room in the boardinghouse where she lives building beautiful but very fictional webs. Learners can discuss what's real and what's not in Sophie's story.

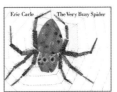

Title: *The Very Busy Spider*
Author: Eric Carle
Suggested Grade Levels: K–2

Summary: A spider patiently tries to build a web while all the other animals on the farm try to distract her.

Conversation Starters:
1. Where does the spider start her web?
2. What pattern does the spider use in making her web?
3. Does she go all the way around the outside first? Go from the outside in? Go back and forth?
4. What did the spider catch in her web?
5. What else might spiders catch in their webs?

Title: *Sophie's Masterpiece*
Author: Eileen Spinelli
Suggested Grade Levels: K–3

Summary: Sophie the spider lives in a boardinghouse. She goes from room to room spinning beautiful creations, but no one appreciates them.

Conversation Starters:

1. Where have you seen spiderwebs? Along walls? On clothes? On trees?
2. Spider silk is beautiful and strong. People have tried to make things from it, but because spiders can only produce so much, it's difficult to get enough spider silk to make even a single piece of clothing. If you had unlimited amounts of spider silk, what would you build?
3. What was Sophie's masterpiece?
4. What happened to Sophie at the end of the story?

REFERENCES AND NONFICTION RESOURCES

Murawski, D. 2004. *Spiders and Their Webs*. Washington, DC: National Geographic Society.

FAST SURFACES
EXPERIMENTING WITH FRICTION

Learners create art with marbles and paint while exploring friction. Kindergarten through second-grade learners will conduct an experiment to test the relative friction of different surfaces. In third and fourth grades, learners will conduct a more complex version of the experiment. Fifth- and sixth-grade learners will also design their own data collection log.

Essential Questions
- What is friction?
- How does friction vary between different surfaces?

Science Background for Educators

Friction is a force that resists motion by giving things grip. One aspect that impacts friction is the texture of objects. For example, the bumps and ridges on a shoe sole help increase friction because the bumps on the shoe sole and the bumps on the ground rub against one another, increasing grip. If the ground were very smooth, like an ice rink, and the shoe sole very smooth, like an ice skate, the friction would be much less, allowing a person to glide along the surface. However, there would still be friction—whenever objects touch each other, there is friction.

In fact, when the surfaces of each object touch, their molecules come in contact with each other and form tiny bonds. As the two surfaces slide apart, the bonds break, and the molecules form new bonds. This process generates heat. When you rub your hands together, this process of molecules forming bonds, the bonds ripping apart, then the bonds re-forming happens over and over and generates the heat you feel in your palms.

There are several different kinds of friction. *Static friction* is exerted by a still object, such as a book on a table. The book will move only when the force of a push or pull is greater than the force of the static friction.

Kinetic friction is generated when an object moves. It might take a lot of force to get an object moving, but once it is moving, less force is needed to keep it in motion. In other words, an object's static friction is greater than its kinetic friction. If that book on the table were set down on top of several rollers, such as a bunch of pencils side by side, it would be much easier to push the book across the table.

★ **COLLABORATION TIP**

Learners should have the opportunity to design their own experiments. After being introduced to the topic of friction in the school library, learners can work in groups to design and conduct their own friction experiments in the classroom to test one or more variables. When the experiments have been completed, school librarians can help learners communicate their results on posters and present their experiments and findings to each other or to parents and community members as part of a mini science fair.

National Standards

Grade Level	AASL Standards Framework for Learners	Next Generation Science Standards: Science and Engineering Practices	National Core Arts Anchor Standards
K–2	I.A.2. Learners display curiosity and initiative by recalling prior and background knowledge as context for new meaning. I.B.1. Learners engage with new knowledge by following a process that includes using evidence to investigate questions. V.C.1. Learners engage with the learning community by expressing curiosity about a topic of personal interest or curricular relevance. I.D.3. Learners participate in an ongoing inquiry-based process by enacting new understanding through real-world connections.	**Practice 1. Asking Questions and Defining Problems** • Ask questions based on observations to find more information about the natural and/or designed world(s). **Practice 3. Planning and Carrying Out Investigations** • Make observations (firsthand or from media) and/or measurements to collect data that can be used to make comparisons.	Anchor Standard 1. Generate and conceptualize artistic ideas and work.
3–4 5–6		**Practice 1. Asking Questions and Defining Problems** • Ask questions that can be investigated and predict reasonable outcomes based on patterns such as cause and effect relationships. **Practice 3. Planning and Carrying Out Investigations** • Make observations and/or measurements to produce data to serve as the basis for evidence for an explanation of a phenomenon or test a design solution.	

Materials

- Shallow box or box lid (1 per group)
- White construction paper (1 sheet per group)
- Cardboard, cut into even lengths to make ramps (3 per group)
- Various surfaces with different textures to test (e.g., felt, aluminum foil, sandpaper, cloth)
- Tape
- Stack of books to create height (1 per group)
- Marbles
- Paint
- *Optional*: Newspaper to cover tables

Preparation

Cover each ramp in a set with a different type of material, taping it down. Repeat so there is one set of ramps per group of learners.

Activity

 THINK

1. Ask learners to rub their hands together. Ask them what they notice. Explain that what they feel is an example of friction—the force between two surfaces. Explain that today learners are going to explore friction.

 CREATE AND SHARE

2. Form groups of learners and give each group a set of cardboard ramps, a tray or box lid, a piece of white construction paper, and a set of marbles.
3. Help learners to set up their experiment by taping the construction paper to the bottom of the box, then putting the ramps side by side so that the lower end is in the tray or box and the upper end is leaning against a stack of books. The paper should extend out and away from the ramps (figure 3.13).
4. When groups are ready, place a small blob of paint at the bottom of each ramp so that each surface is associated with a different color.

FIGURE 3.13

EXPERIMENT SETUP

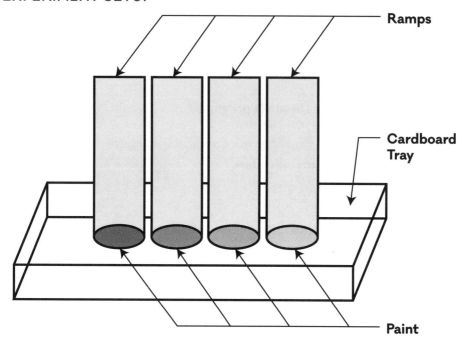

Ramps

Cardboard Tray

Paint

5. Model for learners how to roll a marble down the ramp so that it passes through the paint and creates a trail on the paper.

6. Ask third- and fourth-grade learners and fifth- and sixth-grade learners what information they should collect and how they could collect it. Guide them to create a data collection log.

7. Ask kindergarten through second-grade learners to roll their marbles down the first ramp, observing the result. Note learners' observations on the board.

8. Ask third- and fourth-grade and fifth- and sixth-grade learners to roll their marbles down each ramp one at a time, noting their observations on their logs after each trial.

9. When each ramp has been explored, discuss learners' observations. Which surface has the most friction? The least friction? How do you know?

10. Ask fifth- and sixth-grade learners to repeat the experiment with clean marbles, this time raising or lowering the height of the ramps. What changed? Why?

11. Set aside the ramps and books for the next class.

12. Give learners time to create a piece of art with the marbles and paint within the tray or box by rolling. Ask learners to experiment with the angle of the tray or box. How does the angle affect how fast the marbles roll and the resulting paint trail? Remind learners to keep the marbles and paint in the box.

GROW

13. When learners are done, set aside their art to dry so the trays or box lids can be reused with the next class.
14. Ask learners how friction relates to their everyday life. Where do they see friction in the things they do during the day?

Assessment

Ask learners to draw a picture depicting an example of friction in their everyday life.

Technology Integration

In this Technology Integration, learners collect data in a Google Sheet to predict the relative friction of different surfaces by creating a bar graph. Older learners will decide what data to collect and how best to graph their data.

Before Exploration

1. Create a new Google Sheet (see "Create a New Sheet" in the appendix).
2. For columns A through C, add the following headings, respectively: "Surface Number," "Surface Description," and "Friction."

Exploration

Kindergarten through Second Grade

Before completing the activity, ask learners how friction varies between surfaces and how this variation could slow down an object or allow it to move fast. Show learners how they will be rolling a marble down each surface and across paint to explore friction. Ask them to guess how the different surfaces will affect the distance the marble will travel. Ask them what data they could collect to compare the surfaces, helping them to consider distance as a way to measure the relative friction of a surface.

After learners have completed the activity, help them to transfer their data into the spreadsheet as a class. After they have entered the data, show them how to select the data (columns B and C) and click the Insert Chart button and then choose the column chart (see "Column Chart or Bar Chart" in the appendix). Show learners that the bar graph being displayed is not accurate—they must first check the box to switch rows and columns. Help them fix their graph and interpret the data to determine which surface has the most and least friction.

Third and Fourth Grades

Before completing the activity, explain that learners will be measuring relative friction. Show them how they will explore the concept of friction with marbles, ramps, and paint. Ask them to open a Google Sheet and consider what headings they should use to collect data (i.e., surface description, distance).

After learners have completed the activity and collected their data, have them record their data into the Google Sheet. Ask them to explore the Insert Chart button to answer this question: How do different surfaces affect the distance the marble travels? Encourage learners to justify their conclusions by using data from the graph to support their ideas.

Fifth and Sixth Grades

Repeat the third- and fourth-grade Exploration, but this time have learners create their own headings and collect their own data in groups to answer this question: What is the relationship between the various surfaces and friction? Learners may want to use the words *linear* (straight line), *nonlinear* (curved line), or *proportional* (for every change in roughness, there is a direct change in distance traveled). Have learners share the data their group chose to collect, how they graphed the data, and what their graph says about the relationship between surfaces and friction.

Suggested Picture Books

These suggested picture books address friction and its impact in a variety of circumstances. In *Slow Down, Sara!* learners read about how friction can help people go fast or slow depending on their objective. *On Impact!* introduces the scientific terms *redundancy, inertia,* and *drag* in the context of exploring how a young man could have avoided a bike accident.

....

Title: *Slow Down, Sara!*
Author: Laura Driscoll
Suggested Grade Levels: 1–2

Summary: Sara uses science to make her soapbox racer faster in an effort to win the race.

Conversation Starters:
1. Why did Ben think Sara should slow down?
2. Why did Ben win against Sara when they were gliding their bikes downhill? When they were swimming?
3. What was different about Sara's racer?
4. How was Sara thinking like a scientist?

Title: *On Impact!* (Alien in My Pocket 4)
Author: Nate Ball
Suggested Grade Levels: 1–4

Summary: After Zack is injured in a bicycle accident, he is annoyed by Amp, the alien that crash-landed in Zack's room with scientific information that could have helped him.

Conversation Starters (related to the first fifteen pages of the book):

1. Why does Olivia suggest that Zack should have dragged his feet on the ground? What would that action have done?
2. What does *redundancy* mean? How would it have helped Zack?
3. What is inertia? How is Zack exhibiting inertia?

REFERENCES AND NONFICTION RESOURCES

Mullins, M. 2012. *Friction*. New York, NY: Children's Press.

MELTED CRAYONS
STATES OF MATTER

Learners will explore states of matter by creating melted crayon art using silicone molds. Kindergarten through second-grade learners will investigate how matter changes state. Third- and fourth-grade learners will add the concept of melting point to the investigation. Fifth- and sixth-grade learners will also measure the volume of the crayons before and after melting.

Essential Questions
- How do liquids and solids differ?
- How does matter change state?

Science Background for Educators

Everything around us, even air, is composed of matter. Matter is made up of particles called *atoms,* which can join to form molecules. Particles are always moving.

There are three states of matter: solid, liquid, and gas.

Solids are substances that keep their shape. Liquids are substances that flow; they have no definite shape but will flow to the lowest possible point such as the bottom of a container. Gases are substances that fill a space and flow to match the shape of the space. A gas in a bottle will fill the bottle. A gas in a bottle with no lid will escape the bottle and disperse into the air.

In a solid, each particle is strongly attached to the particles around it, forming a tight mesh. Some solids are malleable and can be stretched into new shapes. In these objects, the matter can be stretched or bent because the molecules can curl and uncurl before they break.

In a liquid, the particles are close together but do not form permanent bonds as in a solid. Because their particles are less packed together, most liquids have lower densities than solids.

In a gas, the particles travel at high speed, bouncing off each other. Because of the spaces between their particles, gases have lower densities than solids and liquids.

Most substances can change from one state of matter to another based on the conditions. For example, water can be a liquid (water), a solid (ice), or a gas (water vapor). A change from one state of matter to another is the result of a change in either temperature or pressure.

National Standards

Grade Level	AASL Standards Framework for Learners	Next Generation Science Standards: Science and Engineering Practices	National Core Arts Anchor Standards
K–2	I.A.2. Learners display curiosity and initiative by recalling prior and background knowledge as context for new meaning. I.B.1. Learners engage with new knowledge by following a process that includes using evidence to investigate questions. I.B.3. Learners engage with new knowledge by following a process that includes generating products that illustrate learning. I.D.3. Learners participate in an ongoing inquiry-based process by enacting new understanding through real-world connections.	**Practice 3. Planning and Carrying Out Investigations** • With guidance, plan and conduct an investigation in collaboration with peers (for K). • Plan and conduct an investigation collaboratively to produce data to serve as the basis for evidence to answer a question. **Practice 4. Analyzing and Interpreting Data** • Use and share pictures, drawings, and/or writings of observations.	Anchor Standard 10. Synthesize and relate knowledge and personal experiences to make art.
3–4		**Practice 3. Planning and Carrying Out Investigations**	
5–6	I.A.2. Learners display curiosity and initiative by recalling prior and background knowledge as context for new meaning. I.B.1. Learners engage with new knowledge by following a process that includes using evidence to investigate questions. I.B.3. Learners engage with new knowledge by following a process that includes generating products that illustrate learning. V.C.2. Learners engage with the learning community by co-constructing innovative means of investigation. I.D.3. Learners participate in an ongoing inquiry-based process by enacting new understanding through real-world connections.	• Plan and conduct an investigation collaboratively to produce data to serve as the basis for evidence, using fair tests in which variables are controlled and the number of trials considered. • Make observations and/or measurements to produce data to serve as the basis for evidence for an explanation of a phenomenon or test a design solution. **Practice 4. Analyzing and Interpreting Data** • Analyze and interpret data to make sense of phenomena, using logical reasoning, mathematics, and/or computation. **Practice 5. Using Mathematics and Computational Thinking** • Describe, measure, estimate, and/or graph quantities (e.g., area, volume, weight, time) to address scientific and engineering questions and problems.	

COLLABORATION TIP

Learners can complete this activity in the school library either after exploring the water cycle in the classroom or as a precursor to a classroom unit on states of matter. Either way, learners can create art with their new crayons. Because this activity can be done with older pieces of crayon that are too small to be held in the fingers, it can also be used as part of a reuse and recycle unit.

Materials

- Crayons, peeled and broken into small pieces
- Silicone molds
- Toothpick or disposable plastic knife
- Microwave*
- Whole crayon
- Hot glue gun
- Hair dryer

- Cardboard
- Newspaper
- Various objects (or images of objects) that are solid and liquid
- Thermometer
- Graduated cylinders (1 per group)**
- Aluminum foil
- Black marker

*If you don't have access to a microwave in the school library or classroom, a hot plate can be used instead. If using a hot plate, place a heat-safe bowl on the hot plate and add water. Heat water to a simmer. Put the crayons into individual silicone molds, aluminum cups, or clean tin cans and place in the water bath until melted. Be careful removing the hot crayon from the water bath.

**If you don't have access to graduated cylinders, learners can use a fairly precise measuring cup.

Preparation

Prior to this lesson, hot glue a crayon to a piece of cardboard. During the activity, use newspaper to protect the space around the cardboard from melted crayon. You may wish to soak the crayons in water for one to two hours; this will make it easier to remove the paper. You can break the crayons into small pieces using a cutting board and knife, or place the crayons in a plastic bag and break them up with a hammer. Of course, do this part on your own, away from learners.

Activity

 THINK

1. Show kindergarten through second-grade learners the water and ice (or a picture of each). Ask learners how the water becomes ice. What has to happen for the ice to turn into water? Ask learners if there are objects other than water that change from a liquid to a solid or vice versa. Explain that learners will explore that process today.

2. Show learners the crayon glued to the cardboard. Ask learners what they have to do to melt the crayon. If needed, remind them of how ice is melted (heat). Show learners the hair dryer and explain that hot air comes out of the hair dryer. Let them feel the hot air on a low setting.

3. Ask learners to observe as you heat up the crayon with the hair dryer. Be sure to angle the hair dryer downward so the wax will melt downward. Ask learners to describe what is happening. After some wax has melted, turn off the dryer. Ask learners to observe what happens after the heat is removed. In a few minutes, the wax should be solid again.

4. With third- and fourth-grade learners, introduce the idea of a melting point and explain that it is the temperature at which an object changes from a solid to a liquid.

5. Ask fifth- and sixth-grade learners if the crayon takes up the same amount of space when it is solid and when it is liquid. Explain that today learners will experiment to make that determination.

 CREATE AND SHARE

6. Explain that today learners will use heat to melt crayons and then allow the crayons to reharden into solids. Fifth- and sixth-grade learners will measure the volume of the crayons when they are solid and when they are liquid.

7. With fifth- and sixth-grade learners:
   a. Explain that the volume of a solid object is the height times the weight times the length of the object. However, objects that don't have flat sides can be hard to measure that way, so another way to measure volume is by displacement.
   b. Demonstrate how to measure the volume of the crayons by filling a graduated cylinder with a specified amount of water, adding the crayons to the water, measuring the resulting volume, and then subtracting the two water measurements to get the volume of the crayons.
   c. Form groups of learners and provide each group with a small cup of crayon bits, a beaker of water, a graduated cylinder, and some paper towels. Guide learners through the process of measuring and recording the volume of their crayons.

    d. Ask learners to remove the crayons from the water and dry them on the paper towels.

    e. Explain that next learners will melt their crayons and measure the volume of the resulting liquid. Ask learners how they might measure the volume of the liquid crayon.

    f. Explain that measuring the volume of a liquid is as simple as pouring it into a vessel that has a volume marking on it, like the graduated cylinder. In this case, however, learners shouldn't pour hot crayon because it's unsafe.

    g. Guide learners to the idea that they can make their own scale, as on the graduated cylinder, for the silicone mold. Give groups a piece of aluminum foil and a black marker. Have learners fold the aluminum foil until it is the shape of a ruler and fairly firm.

    h. Have learners pour 5 milliliters of water into the mold and then dip the aluminum foil into the mold. Demonstrate how to mark and label the water level on the foil. Repeat this step until the mold is almost full and learners have a foil ruler (figure 3.14).

    i. Give each group a number, and number each cup in the mold. Have learners place their crayon pieces into their numbered cup in the silicone mold.

FIGURE 3.14

FOIL RULER IN SILICONE MOLD

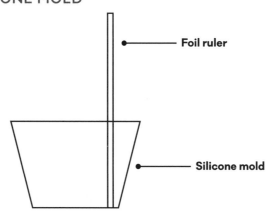

8. Provide crayon pieces and silicone molds to learners and allow them to fill the molds about three-quarters full.

9. Place the molds in the microwave for two minutes, pausing every thirty seconds to stir with a toothpick or disposable plastic knife. Be careful with the hot wax.

As learners are watching, discuss safety and explain that they should not use the microwave at home without parental permission or supervision. Allow learners to observe (without touching) how the crayons change as they melt.

10. During this process, at each stirring point, ask third- and fourth-grade learners to measure the temperature of the crayons and record it on the board. At what temperature were the crayons liquid? That is the melting point of the crayons.

11. When the crayons are fully melted, help fifth- and sixth-grade learners measure the volume of their melted crayons using the foil ruler. To ensure learners' safety, ask learners to watch but not touch the hot crayon or mold. Place learners' foil rulers in the melted crayon for them. The thin layer of wax on the foil should dry quickly and then learners can read it to take and record their measurement.

12. Let the crayons cool, then remove from the mold.

 GROW

13. While the melted crayons are cooling, ask fifth- and sixth-grade learners to compare the volume of their solid and melted crayons. Were the volumes different? Why or why not? Ask learners to predict whether the cooled crayon will have the same volume as the crayon before it was melted. When the crayons are fully cool, have learners follow step 7c again to measure the volume of the cooled crayon and compare all three measurements (before melting, liquid, and after cooling). Explain that matter can change but does not go away. The crayon can be broken into smaller pieces, melted, and cooled, but the matter that is the crayon never goes away.

14. Show kindergarten through second-grade and third- and fourth-grade learners the various items or images of items and ask them to sort whether the items are solid or liquid. How do learners know which is which? Explain that a solid holds its shape whereas a liquid takes the shape of whatever container it is in.

15. Have learners cut pictures from magazines and create a class collage of solid and liquid items.

16. After the crayons have cooled, allow learners to use them to draw a picture that depicts what they learned today.

Assessment

Do learners' drawings reflect an understanding that matter can change states? Ask third- and fourth-grade and fifth- and sixth-grade learners to complete an exit slip with any questions they have.

Technology Integration

Learners use Google Sheets to collect data and graph different states of matter and phase changes through time, using a line and bubble graph.

Before Exploration

1. Create a Google Sheet (see "Create a New Sheet" in the appendix) and add the following column headings to cells A1 through D1, respectively: "State," "Phase," "Time," and "Temperature."
2. In cells F1 through F3, enter "Solid," "Liquid," and "Gas," respectively. In cells G1 through G3, enter "1," "2," and "3," respectively.
3. For cells I1 through L1, enter the following headings, respectively: "Volume Water mL," "Volume Water with Crayon mL," "Calculated Volume of Crayon mL," and "Volume of Melted Crayon mL." You may also want to place this information on a second sheet (see "Adding Sheets" in the appendix).

Exploration

Kindergarten through Second Grade

During step 6 in the Create and Share portion of the activity, display the prepared Google Sheet on the board. Demonstrate how learners will be using "1," "2," and "3" to represent the states of matter: solid, liquid, and gas. Ask learners what images they should insert for water in cells H1 through H3. Show learners how to use Insert Image, and search for a picture to insert in each cell (see "Insert an Image" in the appendix). Tell learners they will be using these numbers to indicate the phase changes for the melting and solidifying of the crayon.

   Designate a learner to be the timekeeper and another learner to be the recorder. As you are melting the crayons in step 9 of the activity, have the timekeeper say "Record" every thirty seconds, at which point the recorder will record the phase of the crayon in the Google Sheet represented by a number. While the crayons are cooling in step 12, demonstrate how to make a graph of these data by selecting the Phase and Time columns and then clicking the Insert Chart button. Choose Line Chart and then remove Time from the items listed under Series (see "Line Chart" in the appendix). Ask learners where a phase change occurred on the graph. Ask learners what was needed to make the phase change.

Third and Fourth Grades

Repeat the kindergarten through second-grade Exploration with the addition of recording temperature data in the temperature column. When graphing, select columns B–D and choose Bubble Chart (see "Bubble Chart" in the appendix). Ask learners what the bubbles are showing. Next, ask where learners think the phase change occurred in the graph.

National Standards

Grade Level	AASL Standards Framework for Learners	Next Generation Science Standards: Science and Engineering Practices	National Core Arts Anchor Standards
K–2	I.A.2. Learners display curiosity and initiative by recalling prior and background knowledge as context for new meaning. I.B.3. Learners engage with new knowledge by following a process that includes generating products that illustrate learning. I.C.1. Learners adapt, communicate, and exchange learning products with others in a cycle that includes interacting with content presented by others. I.D.1. Learners participate in an ongoing inquiry-based process by continually seeking knowledge.	**Practice 5. Using Mathematics and Computational Thinking** • Use counting and numbers to identify and describe patterns in the natural and designed world(s). **Practice 8. Obtaining, Evaluating, and Communicating Information** • Describe how specific images (e.g., a diagram showing how a machine works) support a scientific or engineering idea.	Anchor Standard 1. Generate and conceptualize artistic ideas and work.
3–4 **5–6**	I.A.2. Learners display curiosity and initiative by recalling prior and background knowledge as context for new meaning. III.A.2. Learners identify collaborative opportunities by developing new understandings through engagement in a learning group. I.B.3. Learners engage with new knowledge by following a process that includes generating products that illustrate learning. I.C.1. Learners adapt, communicate, and exchange learning products with others in a cycle that includes interacting with content presented by others. III.C.1. Learners work productively with others to solve problems by soliciting and responding to feedback from others. I.D.1. Learners participate in an ongoing inquiry-based process by continually seeking knowledge.	**Practice 5. Using Mathematics and Computational Thinking** • Organize simple data sets to reveal patterns that suggest relationships. **Practice 6. Constructing Explanations and Designing Solutions** • Use evidence (e.g., measurements, observations, patterns) to construct or support an explanation or design a solution to a problem. • Identify the evidence that supports particular points in an explanation.	

Fifth and Sixth Grades

Share the Google Sheet with each learner (see "Sharing Sheets" in the appendix). During or after step 7 of the activity, ask learners to record their volume of water before and after the crayon in cells I2 and J2. Show learners how to start an equation with an equals sign ("="; see "Equations" in the appendix). Instruct learners to enter an equals sign in cell K2. Demonstrate how to click on a cell, press the Subtract key on the keyboard, then click on another cell to subtract the number in the second cell from the number in the first cell.

After learners have calculated the volume of their crayon, ask learners to record their volumes in a class spreadsheet so that it displays all the volumes. Ask learners what equation might be used to calculate the average volume from all learners. Demonstrate how to use the SUM equation combined with the division symbol ("/") to calculate the average (i.e., =SUM(L1:L3) / 3).

Repeat the preceding actions for the measured volume of the melted crayon. Assist learners in comparing the melted and solid crayon volumes and graph the comparison (see "Choosing and Setting Up Charts" in the appendix). Discuss which type of graph best displays the comparison.

Suggested Picture Books

These suggested picture books address states of matter and how matter changes from one state to another. *Good-bye, Winter! Hello Spring!* follows the water cycle as snow melts, becomes part of the river, flows into the ocean, and eventually becomes clouds and snow once more. Javier and Ana explore states of matter in early spring in *Javier's Hummingbird* as they struggle to keep their hummingbird feeder full of nectar. *In Search of the Fog Zombie* involves a group of campers using science to determine who or what the fog zombie really is.

· ·

Title: *Good-bye, Winter! Hello, Spring!*
Author: Kazuo Iwamura
Suggested Grade Levels: K–3

Summary: When three little squirrels wake up one day, it's spring and the snow is gone. Where did it go?

Conversation Starters:
1. Where did the snow go?
2. Chart the path the water took from puddles on the ground to clouds in the sky.

Title: *Javier's Hummingbird*
Author: Laura Driscoll
Suggested Grade Levels: 1–3

Summary: Javier and Ana feed Rufus the hummingbird and explore solids, liquids, and gases as the nectar in their feeder freezes, melts, and evaporates.

Conversation Starters:
1. In what state of matter is the nectar in the bird feeder?
2. Why didn't the bird initially drink what was in the feeder? What state of matter is ice?
3. Why did the nectar in the feeder turn to ice overnight? Why did it turn back to liquid when Javier brought it inside?
4. What happened to the liquid inside the feeder when the temperature got very hot outside?

Title: *In Search of the Fog Zombie:*
A Mystery about Matter
(Summer Camp Science Mysteries 1)
Author: Lynda Beauregard
Suggested Grade Levels: 3–6

Summary: Angie and Alex and their new friends at Camp Dakota start finding notes about a Fog Zombie. Where will the notes lead?

Conversation Starters:
1. What happens to the water droplets in fog when the sun heats them?
2. Why would Angie have an easier time swimming if she were in the ocean instead of a lake?
3. How did the kids get the message out of the cube of ice?
4. What made the wire get longer? Why did that happen?
5. What explained the "zombie" sounds the kids heard?

REFERENCES AND NONFICTION RESOURCES

Oxlade, C. 2002. *States of Matter.* Chicago, IL: Reed Education and Professional Publishing.
Walker, S. M. 2006. *Matter.* Minneapolis, MN: Lerner.

STRING ART
EXPLORING PATTERNS

Learners will explore patterns while making prints using string and wooden blocks. Kindergarten through second-grade learners will make patterns by rotating their block a quarter turn with each print. Third- and fourth-grade learners will explore how they can work together to include more than one print in their pattern. Fifth- and sixth-grade learners will also work collaboratively to create a more advanced pattern.

Essential Question

- How can one generate and analyze a pattern?

Science Background for Educators

Patterns are part of our everyday life. Not only do they exist in nature (seashells, snowflakes, etc.), but we use them in our technological world as well. Software is used to detect patterns in documents and data to reveal information about the world, and researchers seek out patterns to increase their scientific understanding. Engineers also create patterns in the design of buildings and bridges and roads. These patterns can be aesthetic, and they can also help users of those objects use them more intuitively. For example, if the stairs are in the same place on each floor of the building, they will be easier to find.

 COLLABORATION TIP

After exploring rotating patterns in the school library, learners can continue to explore patterns by creating tessellations, by rotating shapes, and by exploring the patterns present in music with their classroom, art, or music educator.

Materials

- 2-inch wooden blocks (1 per learner)
- String
- Scissors (1 pair per learner)
- Glue
- Paint
- Construction paper*
- Newspaper to protect tables

*To help learners make their block printing accurate, you may wish to draw a 2-inch-by-2-inch grid on the construction paper or help learners to draw their own grid.

Grade Level	AASL Standards Framework for Learners	Next Generation Science Standards: Science and Engineering Practices	National Core Arts Anchor Standards
K–2	I.A.2. Learners display curiosity and initiative by recalling prior and background knowledge as context for new meaning. I.B.3. Learners engage with new knowledge by following a process that includes generating products that illustrate learning. I.C.1. Learners adapt, communicate, and exchange learning products with others in a cycle that includes interacting with content presented by others. I.D.1. Learners participate in an ongoing inquiry-based process by continually seeking knowledge.	**Practice 5. Using Mathematics and Computational Thinking** • Use counting and numbers to identify and describe patterns in the natural and designed world(s). **Practice 8. Obtaining, Evaluating, and Communicating Information** • Describe how specific images (e.g., a diagram showing how a machine works) support a scientific or engineering idea.	Anchor Standard 1. Generate and conceptualize artistic ideas and work.
3–4 5–6	I.A.2. Learners display curiosity and initiative by recalling prior and background knowledge as context for new meaning. III.A.2. Learners identify collaborative opportunities by developing new understandings through engagement in a learning group. I.B.3. Learners engage with new knowledge by following a process that includes generating products that illustrate learning. I.C.1. Learners adapt, communicate, and exchange learning products with others in a cycle that includes interacting with content presented by others. III.C.1. Learners work productively with others to solve problems by soliciting and responding to feedback from others. I.D.1. Learners participate in an ongoing inquiry-based process by continually seeking knowledge.	**Practice 5. Using Mathematics and Computational Thinking** • Organize simple data sets to reveal patterns that suggest relationships. **Practice 6. Constructing Explanations and Designing Solutions** • Use evidence (e.g., measurements, observations, patterns) to construct or support an explanation or design a solution to a problem. • Identify the evidence that supports particular points in an explanation.	

Preparation

Each block should have an arrow scribed on the back so learners can see which way it is pointed when making prints (figure 3.15). There should be two evenly spaced marks on each edge of the front side of the block. Depending on time and learner ability, you may wish to prepare the blocks in advance or you may wish to walk learners through preparing their own blocks.

FIGURE 3.15

PREPARED WOODEN BLOCK

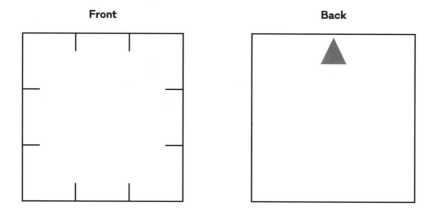

Front   Back

Activity

 THINK

1. Show learners images of painted tile patterns. Explain that people all over the world decorate their homes and buildings with painted tiles. Sometimes the patterns look quite complex but in fact are easy to make if one follows the pattern of turns.
2. Explain that today learners will make their own tile pattern using a form of art called a *print*. Explain what a print is.

 CREATE

3. Provide each learner one prepared wooden block, string, scissors, and glue. Demonstrate how to glue the string onto the wooden block so that the beginning and end of each string lead from a mark on one edge of the block to any other mark (figure 3.16).
4. Direct learners to cover the string in paint and press firmly onto the paper, then carefully pick up the block, rotate it a quarter turn clockwise, and repeat. Keep repeating until the paper is full. Learners may need to apply more paint as they go.

FIGURE 3.16

EXAMPLE OF BLOCK WITH STRINGS

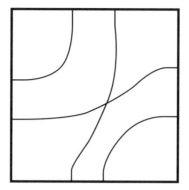

 SHARE

5. Ask third- and fourth-grade and fifth- and sixth-grade learners what would happen if they worked together and used several block patterns on one sheet. Could they make a different kind of pattern? Form groups of learners and provide each group a second sheet of paper. Ask learners to create a new pattern on the new paper using at least two different blocks (third- and fourth-grade learners) and including at least one block rotation (fifth- and sixth-grade learners). Learners may wish to practice on a blank sheet of printer paper.

6. Have learners do a gallery walk to examine each other's prints. What is the same and what is different in the prints?

 GROWTH MINDSET TIP

If learners are struggling, encourage them to use positive self-talk with statements such as "Challenges help me grow" or "I'll try a different strategy."

 GROW

7. Ask learners what would happen if the strings didn't go from one edge to the other on the marks. Would the pattern still work? Why or why not?

8. Ask fifth- and sixth-grade learners what other shapes could be used to make this sort of pattern. Draw a circle, triangle, trapezoid, pentagon, and hexagon on the board as examples. The circle doesn't work because there are no edges to line up, but the other shapes would work.

Assessment

Have each learner use a block to color in one square on a clean grid. Ask more advanced learners to rotate their blocks so that each successive block is rotated a quarter turn clockwise in respect to the block before it. Do the marks on the print line up? Ask learners to explain orally or in writing why this process works.

Technology Integration

Learners use Google Sheets to create a pixel pattern by filling in cells with color using numbers and equations.

Before Exploration

1. Start a new Google Sheet (see "Create a New Sheet" in the appendix). Create a shareable link (see "Sharing Sheets" in the appendix). Change the width and height of all cells to make them square (see "Resizing Rows or Columns" in the appendix).
2. Create a second sheet (see "Create a New Sheet" in the appendix) and generate a shareable link for the new sheet (see "Sharing Sheets" in the appendix). In cells A1 through A10, enter the numbers "2," "4," "6," "8," "10," and "12," respectively. Select all cells and set up conditional formatting so that each number represents a particular color (see "Conditional Formatting" in the appendix).
3. *Optional*: If time is an issue, set up a new sheet for fifth- and sixth-grade learners, placing numbers "1" through "10" in cells A1 through A10, respectively. Select all cells and apply color to the cells using the Greater Than or Less Than rule in the Conditional Formatting menu (figure 3.17). For example, values of 1 and 2 might be orange, values of 3 and 4 might be yellow, values of 5 and 6 might be blue, and so on up to 10. Then, type "1" in D1.

FIGURE 3.17

CONDITIONAL FORMATTING

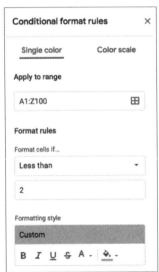

FIGURE 3.18

TRIANGLE IN GOOGLE SHEETS

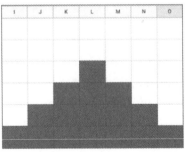

Exploration

Kindergarten through Second Grade

After the activity, share the link to the shared Google Sheet with learners and instruct them to make a copy. Show learners how to make a triangle shape by changing the cells to red using Fill Color (figure 3.18; see "Fill Color" in the appendix).

Next, show learners how to select all the cells that make up the triangle and copy those cells. Demonstrate how to choose a spot somewhere next to the triangle and paste a rotated version of the triangle using Paste Special > Transpose (see "Paste Special / Transpose" in the appendix) from the Edit menu (see "Copying and Pasting Text" in the appendix). Based on what they saw happen and when, ask learners what they think the word *transpose* means. Ask learners to repeat the process to create a pattern with each iteration of their pasted triangle. Learners may want to zoom out and remove gridlines to see their patterns more clearly.

Third and Fourth Grades

After the activity, share the link to the shared Google Sheet with learners and have them make a copy. Demonstrate how the color of the cell changes based on the number typed into the cell. Type "2" in cell G3 and "4" in cell G4. Explain that you will add the two cells and type "6" in cell G5. Ask learners if this math just created a pattern. Give them time to create their own pattern by adding or subtracting numbers from the list, placing the answer in the cell each time. Ask learners if they could repeat that pattern by copying and pasting. Is there a relationship between the numbers and color patterns?

Fifth and Sixth Grades

After the activity, share the prepared Google Sheet with learners, or instruct them on how to create their own using the instructions in step 3 of the "Before Exploration" section. Demonstrate how to enter an equation in cell E1 by typing "=D1+1" and then pressing the Return key. Ask learners to predict what would happen if they repeated that equation down the column to cell E8. Show learners how to select cell D1, grab the square in the lower left corner, and drag down to cell D8 to autofill (see "Autofill" in the appendix). Ask learners to predict what pattern would happen if they entered the equation "=E1-1" in cell F1. Ask learners to repeat the two equations in cells G1 and H1, respectively. Demonstrate how this action creates a pattern. Give learners time to create their own patterns.

Suggested Picture Books

The suggested books address patterns in nature and culture. *Growing Patterns: Fibonacci Numbers in Nature* and *Mysterious Patterns: Finding Fractals in Nature* present information about and examples of these unique mathematical patterns. *Rickshaw Girl* is about Naima, a Bangladeshi girl who loves to paint traditional *alpana* patterns during the holidays.

Title: *Growing Patterns: Fibonacci Numbers in Nature*
Author: Sarah C. Campbell
Suggested Grade Levels: 3–4

Summary: Fibonacci sequences are simple patterns in which each number in the sequence is the sum of the two numbers that come before it. These patterns appear in nature throughout the world in different ways.

Conversation Starters:
1. What is a Fibonacci number?
2. Are all numbers in nature Fibonacci numbers?

Title: *Rickshaw Girl*
Author: Mitali Perkins
Suggested Grade Levels: 3–6

Summary: During the holidays, Bangladeshi women and girls paint *alpana* patterns in their homes. Prizes are given for the best designs, and Naima is hoping to win, but she also wants to earn money to help her family.

Conversation Starters (based on chapter 1 of the book):
1. What are *alpanas*? What does Naima's mother remind her about when she's painting *alpanas*?
2. Why isn't Naima going to school?

Title: *Mysterious Patterns: Finding Fractals in Nature*
Author: Sarah C. Campbell
Suggested Grade Levels: 3–6

Summary: Natural shapes are often rough or bristly; they don't have clean geometric lines. Many of these shapes seem chaotic, but they have a pattern called a *fractal*.

Conversation Starters:
1. What is a fractal pattern?
2. Where can we find fractal patterns in nature?
3. Is every pattern in nature a fractal?

Title: *Spotty, Stripy, Swirly: What Are Patterns?*
Author: Jane Brocket
Suggested Grade Levels: K–2

Summary: Photographs of man-made and natural objects reveal the patterns present throughout our daily lives.

Conversation Starters:
1. How can patterns be helpful?
2. What patterns do you see in the classroom? In the school library?
3. Do you have a favorite pattern?

REFERENCES AND NONFICTION RESOURCES

Brundle, J. 2018. *Patterns*. New York, NY: KidHaven Publishing.

Tang, G. 2001. *The Grapes of Math: Mind-Stretching Math Riddles*. New York, NY: Scholast

CHAPTER 4

Designing Like an Engineer

A s explained in the preceding chapter, "Thinking Like a Scientist," a STEAM approach to the school library curriculum involves science, engineering, and technology. Each discipline shares commonalities but is also distinct. The eight practices of science and engineering (figure 4.1) apply to both scientific and engineering work and align with the *National School Library Standards*. For example, a learner who is developing and using models (NGSS Practice 2) in science might create a physical replica in order to make a prediction about a natural phenomenon. On the other hand, a learner engaged in a design pursuit might use a physical model to determine where or when flaws might develop in the potential solution. Whether devising a model for a scientific or engineering-based activity, learners will be practicing Explore Competencies as they problem-solve through cycles of design, implementation, and reflection (AASL 2018, Learner V.B.1.) or iteratively respond to challenges (AASL 2018, Learner V.D.1.).

A learner who designs like an engineer will use the design process to create solutions to problems. The seven activities in this chapter focus on the skills a learner would employ to design like an engineer. A learner engaged in a design activity might define a problem (Inquire); determine information needed to define the constraints of the problem (Curate); engage in an iterative process of testing, revising, and retesting (Explore); envision the design from multiple viewpoints and seek out varying perspectives (Include); evaluate potential solutions independently (Explore) or collaboratively (Collaborate); and communicate results in a manner appropriate to the audience (Engage).

FIGURE 4.1

ENGINEERING METHOD

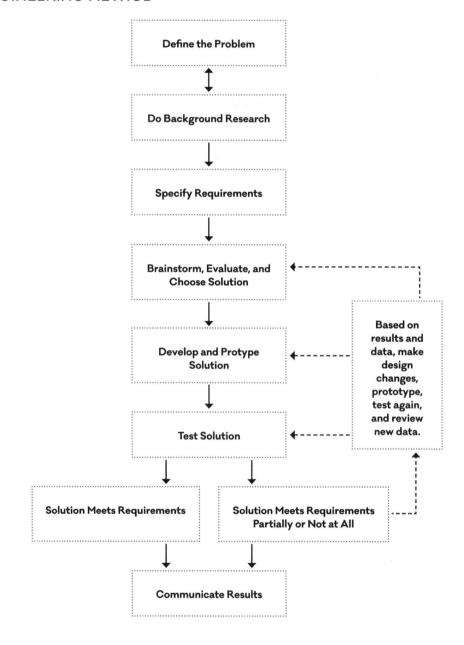

WORKING TOGETHER
BUILD-A-TOWER CHALLENGE

In this activity, learners will explore how working alone versus working together makes a difference in their creative potential. Using simple supplies (string, paper, etc.), learners will be given a short time to build the biggest tower they can with their materials. Then they will repeat the activity in small groups with the same materials and time. The school librarian or classroom educator will guide learners through a discussion of what was different and why, as well as how to overcome some of the challenges of working together. In addition to discussing teamwork in more depth at higher grade levels, third- and fourth-grade learners will be challenged to build a tower that can withstand an earthquake (shaking desk), and fifth- and sixth-grade learners will add the component of working within a budget.

Essential Questions
- What are the advantages of working as a team?
- What skills do you need to be an effective team member?

Science Background for Educators

Since the beginning of human civilization, people have tried to build tall structures. The Egyptians built the Great Pyramid of Giza, which was the tallest man-made structure in the world for almost 4,500 years.

How tall buildings can get is dependent on technology. Initially, most buildings were made of stone. Over time, builders began using metal because it is very strong and can support greater height than stone.

Other innovations had to be made for the first skyscraper to be built. The elevator was necessary to allow easy access to the upper floors of tall buildings. Electricity was needed for adequate lighting. Plumbing and heating were also required for comfort. Finally, communications technologies such as the telephone helped to make skyscrapers useful to all sorts of people.

When a tower, or skyscraper, is built, thousands of people are involved. Before a bulldozer digs the first shovelful of dirt, engineers, architects, and the owners have spent considerable time designing and prototyping the building to ensure that it meets their vision for use and creativity.

Each person has an important role to play in the building process. The owner (usually a company rather than an individual person) decides what the building will be used for and pays for it to be built. The owner will also buy the land, hire the architect, and approve the design.

The architect designs the building. This process includes deciding how tall the building will be, what materials it will be made of (concrete, steel, glass, etc.), and what style it will have.

Various engineers work with the architect to ensure that every part of the building functions as designed. Structural engineers are involved with the frame and foundation of the building. Geotechnical engineers study the soils and rocks in the ground to help the structural engineers make decisions about the building's foundation. Electrical engineers design the electrical systems. Mechanical engineers design the air, heating, and cooling systems. Each of these experts creates blueprints, drawings that show how each piece of the building should be built.

City planners review the building's plans to ensure that they meet city building and safety codes, while surveyors check the property lines and note special features of the property such as slopes, natural drainage areas, and wet areas.

Once all the plans are approved, construction companies are hired to build the skyscraper. The contractor is responsible for all details of the building process, including bringing materials to the site, hiring workers, and keeping everything on schedule.

 COLLABORATION TIP

After learners have explored the power of working together and the basic ideas of the design process in the school library, the classroom educator can build on this lesson by giving learners time in the classroom to continue refining their designs. The educator may choose to impose additional restrictions (such as setting a maximum size for the base of the tower) to make the challenge more complex or address additional scientific or mathematical concepts (e.g., making sure the building doesn't block the sun in the morning).

Materials
- LEGO blocks of various shapes and sizes (1 kit for each learner)
- *Optional*: Tray or box lid (1 per learner)
- Fake money (for fifth- and sixth-grade learners, $25 per group)

Preparation
Divide the LEGOs into kits so that each learner has approximately the same number of LEGOs. For the fifth- and sixth-grade version of this activity, learners should start with fewer LEGOs. They must "buy" additional LEGOs with their budget. The classroom educator should create a pricing chart based on the type of LEGOs available (e.g., $1 for a small LEGO block, $2 for a large LEGO block, etc.)

National Standards

Grade Level	AASL Standards Framework for Learners	Next Generation Science Standards: Science and Engineering Practices	National Core Arts Anchor Standards
K–2	V.A.2. Learners develop and satisfy personal curiosity by reflecting and questioning assumptions and possible misconceptions. V.B.1. Learners construct new knowledge by problem solving through cycles of design, implementation, and reflection. V.C.3. Learners engage with the learning community by collaboratively identifying innovative solutions to a challenge or problem. V.D.2. Learners develop through experience and reflection by recognizing capabilities and skills that can be developed, improved, and expanded.	**Practice 2. Developing and Using Models** • Compare models to identify common features and differences.	Anchor Standard 1. Generate and conceptualize artistic ideas and work. Anchor Standard 7. Perceive and analyze artistic work.
3–4		**Practice 2. Developing and Using Models** • Develop a model using an analogy, example, or abstract representation to describe a scientific principle or design solution.	
5–6			

Activity

 THINK

1. Show learners the kits of LEGO blocks. Ask learners how tall a tower they think they can make with that many LEGO blocks. Explain that third- and fourth-grade and fifth- and sixth-grade learners will be making a tower that can withstand an earthquake. Demonstrate how you will shake the desk to simulate an earthquake.

✖ CREATE

2. Give each learner a set of LEGOs and explain that learners will have five minutes to build a tower as tall as they can. Use the trays or box lids to ensure that each learner has a space to work, or learners can work directly on desks and tables.
3. Explain the rules:
    a. The tower must be freestanding, meaning it's standing up without anyone holding it up or anything else supporting it.
    b. Learners may use only the LEGO pieces they are given—no sharing or trading.
    c. If a learner's tower falls, the learner can start over but will still have only five minutes from start to finish.

4. When time is up, gently shake the table of each third- and fourth-grade and fifth- and sixth-grade learner to see if their tower can withstand the movement. Ask learners if they were able to build their tower as tall as they thought. Why or why not?
5. Explain that learners will repeat the activity, but this time they will work in groups; fifth- and sixth-grade learners will also add a budget component. Form groups of learners and explain that they should combine their LEGOs. They can take apart the towers they already made if they need the LEGO pieces. For fifth- and sixth-grade groups, explain that when engineers are designing structures like skyscrapers, they have a budget to work with—that is, they have a defined amount of money they can spend on the materials for the project. Learners will be simulating this aspect by starting with only a few LEGOs. They may then buy additional LEGOs with their $25 of fake money. Show learners the pricing chart and give each group $25.
6. Remind learners of the rules:
    a. The tower must be freestanding, meaning it's standing up without anyone holding it up or anything else supporting it.
    b. Learners may use only the LEGO pieces they are given or purchase (for fifth- and sixth-grade learners)—no sharing or trading with other groups.
    c. If a group's tower falls, the group can start over, but they still have only five minutes from start to finish.

7. When time is up, gently shake the tables of the third- and fourth-grade and fifth- and sixth-grade learners to see if their tower can withstand the movement.
8. Ask learners if their towers were taller after working with a group. Why or why not? Ask fifth- and sixth-grade learners how they decided what to spend money on. Did the money make the task easier or harder? Why?

SHARE

9. Allow learners a few minutes to look at the other groups' towers. Ask them to describe what they notice. Who made the tallest tower? Which towers show a lot of creativity? Now that they have seen what other groups built, what ideas would they use to improve on their tower?

 GROW

10. As a group, discuss the results of the two iterations of the activity. What was different between working alone and working in a group? What part of the activity was the easiest? What part was the hardest?

11. Explain that one engineer could never design and build a skyscraper all alone. Architects, owners, and engineers work together to determine the building's location and design. The architect designs the skyscraper, deciding on the style and building materials. There are different types of engineers, and each one works with the architect on a specific component of the building. Some work on the electricity, others on the heating and air conditioning systems. Some work on the frame and foundation of the building. Of course, there are also contractors who manage the construction, builders who work for the contractors to build the building, and lots of other people who help complete the project. Everyone must do their part. (See the "Science Background for Educators" and "References and Nonfiction Resources" sections for additional information.)

12. Ask learners to think back on what they did during the activity. How could they have been a better teammate? As a class, make a list of the qualities of a good teammate. How would those qualities have helped them make a better tower?

 GROWTH MINDSET TIP
Remind learners that improving on a skill doesn't mean you are bad at it now; everyone has room for improvement!

Assessment

Provide each learner with a sheet of paper titled "teamwork contract." Ask learners to record one thing they will do to become a better teammate, then have them write their name at the bottom.

Technology Integration

Using Google Sheets, learners collect data and rate bridges built with LEGOs to determine the effects of working together.

Before Exploration

1. Create a Google Sheet with the following headings in row 2: "Height," "Strength Rating," "Cost," "Height," "Strength Rating," and "Cost" (see "Create a New Sheet" in the appendix).
2. In row 1, merge cells A1 through C1 and repeat for cells D1 through F1 (see "Formatting Text or Cells and Menu Options" in the appendix). Title the first merged cell "Alone" and the second "Group."
3. Create a Strength Legend in column H by adding icons to the cells (see "Insert an Icon" in the appendix).
4. Add a sheet and rename the sheet "Team Roles" (see "Adding Sheets" in the appendix). Add the following roles to row 1 of columns A through E: "Leader," "Builder," "Timekeeper," "Materials Helper," and "Positive Idea Helper." Add a checkbox to cell A2 (see "Insert a Checkbox" in the appendix) and then copy the cell to fill five or six rows under the column headings (figure 4.2).

FIGURE 4.2

TEAM ROLES

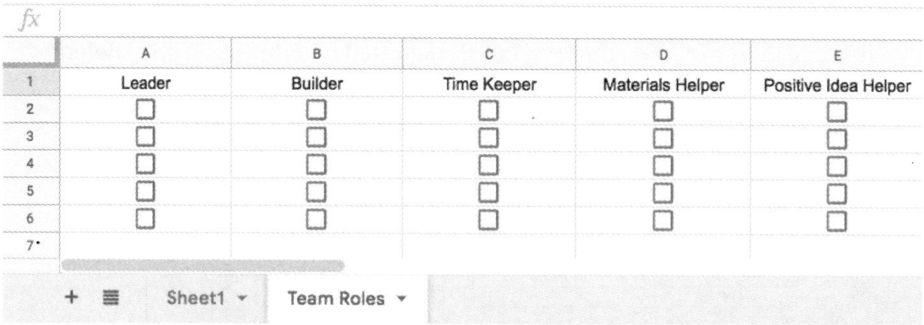

Exploration

Kindergarten through Second Grade

Before step 4 of the activity, ask each learner to measure the height of their LEGO tower.

After learners have built their LEGO towers in groups in step 5 of the activity, ask groups to once again measure the height of their towers. Send one learner from each group to the computer to enter the group's data. After all data are entered, select column A and generate a column chart (see "Column Chart or Bar Chart" in the appendix). Repeat for column E.

Ask learners if the height of their towers improved when they worked together. What about strength? Turn to the Team Roles sheet in the Google Sheet and instruct learners to go to the computer and check the box under the role they played in their group (figure 4.3). Ask learners if some roles should be played by more people. Why or why not?

FIGURE 4.3

WORKING TOGETHER DATA

	A	B	C	D	E	F	G	H
1	**Team Roles**							
2	Leader	☐	☑	☐	☐	☐	☐	☐
3	Builder	☐	☐	☐	☑	☐	☐	☐
4	Time Keeper	☑	☐	☐	☐	☐	☐	☐
5	Materials Helper	☐	☐	☐	☐	☐	☐	☐
6	Positive Idea Hel	☐	☑	☐	☐	☐	☑	☐

Third and Fourth Grades

Before step 4 of the activity, show learners the strength scale and ask them to agree as a class on what each rating means. For example, one arm might mean the structure fell down when shaking, and four arms means it withstood a lot of shaking.

Repeat the kindergarten through second-grade Exploration, individually and then in groups. When learners choose their team role, ask them to select the main role they played so that each learner is choosing only one role. In the row under the checkboxes, add the number of checked boxes and record the number. Compare the values. Ask learners if all roles are needed for a strong tower. Why or why not?

Fifth and Sixth Grades

Follow the instructions for third- and fourth-grade learners; however, this time ask learners to also report if they used a lot of money or little money in the cost columns. After all data are entered, demonstrate how to use the Explore button to generate charts (see "Explore Button" in the appendix). Ask learners to use graphs to answer the following questions: Is there a correlation between the strength of a tower and money spent? Is there a correlation between the strength and height of a tower? How about building alone compared to building together?

Suggested Picture Books

The suggested picture books are focused on the theme of teamwork. Each book demonstrates an advantage of working together with others. In *Cook-a-Doodle-Doo!* Rooster shares his knowledge of baking with a team of animals who help him build a cake. In *Lady Pancake and Sir French Toast,* two friends learn that they can accomplish more working together than when they compete. In *The Mouse Who Reached the Sky,* a mouse recognizes that he can't accomplish his goal on his own and must get help.

....

Title: *Cook-a-Doodle-Doo!*
Author: Janet Stevens and Susan Stevens Crummel
Suggested Grade Levels: K–3

Summary: Rooster wants to bake a cake, so he recruits Pig, Iguana, and Turtle to help, but none of his friends know how to cook. With Rooster's help, they learn how to cook.

Conversation Starters:
1. What did each animal agree to do to help make the cake?
2. How did the animals work together as a team?
3. Why do you think making the cake was much easier the second time?

Title: *Lady Pancake and Sir French Toast*
Author: Josh Funk
Suggested Grade Levels: K–6

Summary: Lady Pancake and Sir French Toast are good friends, but when they hear that there is only one drop of syrup left, a competition to reach it begins.

Conversation Starters:
1. What starts the race to the syrup?
2. How do Lady Pancake and Sir French Toast treat each other during the competition?
3. Why does neither of them get the syrup? What should they have done differently?

Title: *The Mouse Who Reached the Sky*
Author: Petr Horáček
Suggested Grade Levels: K–1

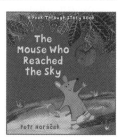

Summary: Mouse spots a shiny red thing in a tree, but he can't reach it, so he goes to get help.

Conversation Starters:
1. Why did Mouse need help to get the shiny red thing?
2. What did each character (Mouse, Mole, and Rabbit) think the shiny red thing was? What was it really?
3. How did the three of them finally get the cherries?
4. What could they have done instead of climbing on top of each other to reach the fruit?

REFERENCES AND NONFICTION RESOURCES

Curlee, L. 2007. *Skyscraper*. New York, NY: Simon and Schuster.

Johmann, C. A. 2001. *Skyscrapers! Super Structures to Design and Build*. Charlotte, VT: Williamson Publishing.

BUILDING A FLASHLIGHT
LOOKING AT CIRCUITS

Learners explore circuits by building their own flashlight using batteries, paper clips, light bulbs, paper towel rolls, and other household materials. After dissecting a flashlight as a whole class and discussing the role of insulators and conductors, kindergarten through second-grade learners will test which objects will light up a bulb when placed between a battery and the bulb, using aluminum foil as a conductor. Third- and fourth-grade learners will be given the materials to make a basic circuit and will create one through experimentation. Fifth- and sixth-grade learners will create a working flashlight using the provided materials.

Essential Question
- How does a circuit work?

Science Background for Educators

Electricity travels through circuits. When you connect a battery to a light bulb, it creates a circuit, or a closed path that allows the current to flow from the positive terminal to the negative terminal of the battery. The voltage of the battery pushes electrons through the circuit, including the filament inside the light bulb. As the electrons travel through the filament, the resistance makes the filament so hot that it generates light.

In order for the circuit to work, it must be a closed circuit, meaning there is no break between the source of power and the electric device, such as a battery and bulb in a flashlight (figure 4.4). A switch allows the circuit to be open (off) or closed (on) by connecting and disconnecting the two wires (figure 4.5).

FIGURE 4.4

OPEN AND CLOSED CIRCUITS

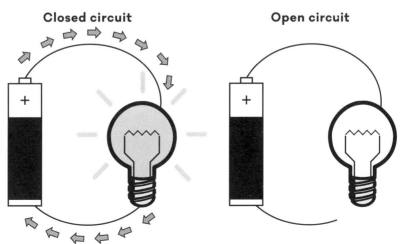

Closed circuit   Open circuit

FIGURE 4.5

CIRCUIT WITH SWITCH

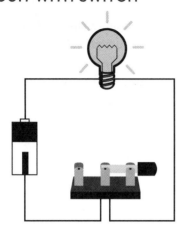
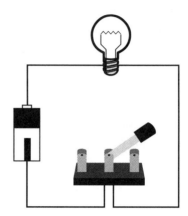

> ★ **COLLABORATION TIP**
>
> During the activity, learners will not have sufficient time to plan, prototype, and refine their designs for a flashlight. After building a basic, functioning flashlight, learners can continue this investigation in the classroom by continuing to refine their flashlight to make it brighter, easier to use, or more aesthetically pleasing.

Materials

- Wire stripper
- 1 string of holiday lights (Cut the string apart, leaving 3 inches of wire on each end. Strip 1 inch of coating from the end of each wire, then twist the wire strands together.)
- D batteries (1 per pair of learners)
- Cardboard tubes from paper towel rolls (1 per pair of learners)
- Scissors to share
- Light bulbs, 3-volt (1 per pair of learners)
- Insulated copper wire, 22-gauge, cut into 10-inch lengths (1 length per pair of learners)
- Duct tape to share
- Paper clips
- Aluminum foil
- Small plastic or paper drink cups
- Various art supplies
- Pencil

National Standards

Grade Level	AASL Standards Framework for Learners	Next Generation Science Standards: Science and Engineering Practices	National Core Arts Anchor Standards
K–2	I.B.1. Learners engage with new knowledge by following a process that includes using evidence to investigate questions. IV.A.1. Learners act on an information need by determining the need to gather information. V.B.1. Learners construct new knowledge by problem solving through cycles of design, implementation, and reflection. V.C.3. Learners engage with the learning community by collaboratively identifying innovative solutions to a challenge or problem.	**Practice 4. Analyzing and Interpreting Data** • Analyze data from tests of an object or tool to determine if it works as intended. **Practice 6. Constructing Explanations and Designing Solutions** • Make observations (firsthand or from media) to construct an evidence-based account for natural phenomena.	Anchor Standard 1. Generate and conceptualize artistic ideas and work.
3–4	I.B.1. Learners engage with new knowledge by following a process that includes using evidence to investigate questions. IV.A.1. Learners act on an information need by determining the need to gather information. V.B.1. Learners construct new knowledge by problem solving through cycles of design, implementation, and reflection. V.D.1. Learners develop through experience and reflection by iteratively responding to challenges.	**Practice 3. Planning and Carrying Out Investigations** • Make observations and/or measurements to produce data to serve as the basis for evidence for an explanation of a phenomenon or test a design solution. **Practice 6. Constructing Explanations and Designing Solutions** • Apply scientific ideas to solve design problems.	
5–6		**Practice 3. Planning and Carrying Out Investigations** • Plan and conduct an investigation collaboratively to produce data to serve as the basis for evidence, using fair tests in which variables are controlled and the number of trials considered. **Practice 6. Constructing Explanations and Designing Solutions** • Generate and compare multiple solutions to a problem based on how well they meet the criteria and constraints of the design solution.	

Activity

 THINK

1. Show learners a flashlight. Ask them what makes the flashlight light up. Ask learners how they could find out.
2. Talk about the different parts of the flashlight: bulb, tube, battery, switch.
3. Form pairs of third- and fourth-grade learners and fifth- and sixth-grade learners. Give each pair a battery and a holiday light. Ask learners to spend a few minutes exploring. How can they get the bulb to light up? What works? What doesn't? Explain the concepts of a closed circuit and an open circuit. Explain how energy flows from the battery into the light bulb, converting electrical current to light, when the circuit is closed.

 CREATE

4. Take a length of wire and show kindergarten through second-grade learners how the wire and battery can be used to light up the bulb. Add another length of wire and ask learners if they think the light will shine if a pencil is placed between the two wires (figure 4.6). Explain that the electricity that flows from the battery to the light can flow through some objects but not through others.

FIGURE 4.6

CONDUCTIVITY TESTING

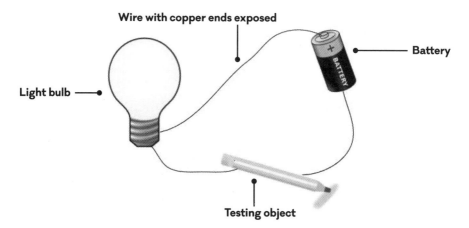

Wire with copper ends exposed

Battery

Light bulb

Testing object

5. Show kindergarten through second-grade learners a variety of items (aluminum foil, cardboard tube, rock, penny, etc.) and ask them how they can find out which items will allow electricity to pass through—in other words, which items can they place between the two wires and still have the bulb light up. As a class or in groups, test each item, recording learners' predictions and actual results on a piece of chart paper.

---

6. Give third- and fourth-grade and fifth- and sixth-grade learner pairs a light bulb, two batteries, a length of wire, and a cardboard tube from a paper towel roll. Ask learners to make a simple flashlight using the same principle they used to make the holiday light illuminate, except on a larger scale. As they try different things, redirect them to think about the battery and holiday light. How can they re-create that idea with these other objects?

 GROWTH MINDSET TIP
As needed, remind learners that design is not easy and takes time. Part of the design process is trial and error; not everything will work.

7. If time permits, ask third- and fourth-grade learners to enhance their flashlight. How can they make the light shine more effectively using the remaining supplies?
8. Ask fifth- and sixth-grade learners to modify their flashlights to include a switch so the flashlights can be turned on and off. Provide learners with additional materials such as paper clips and foil for use in designing their switch.

 SHARE AND GROW

9. Remind kindergarten through second-grade learners that the electricity that flows from the battery to the light can flow through some objects but not through others.
10. Have third- and fourth-grade and fifth- and sixth-grade pairs join another pair and compare their flashlights and the process they used to design them. What worked and what didn't?

Assessment

For kindergarten through second-grade learners, refer to the chart paper and ask learners which objects enable electricity to flow through them. For third- and fourth-grade learners, listen to their explanations of what worked and what didn't in step 10 or ask them to write down those explanations. Do their explanations reflect an understanding of open and closed circuits?

Technology Integration

Learners use Google Sheets to identify the process for building a flashlight while evaluating each attempt in the design process.

Before Exploration

1. Create a new Google Sheet (see "Create a New Sheet" in the appendix). Add a new sheet (see "Adding Sheets" in the appendix).
2. Rename Sheet1 "K–2." Label column A "Flashlight Part," column B "Step," column H "Conductive Material," and column I "Light?". In cells B2 through B5, enter "1," "2," "3," and "4." In cells C2 through F2, insert images of a light bulb, battery, wire, and lens (see "Insert an Image" in the appendix). Resize rows A2 through A5 so they can later accommodate the images that were just added to the sheet (see "Resizing Rows or Columns" in the appendix; figure 4.7).

FIGURE 4.7

K–2 SHEET

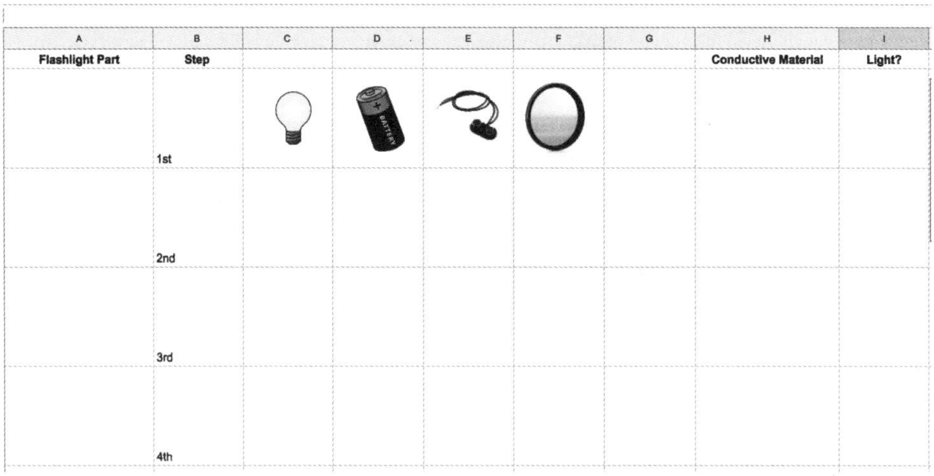

A	B	C	D	E	F	G	H	I
Flashlight Part	Step						Conductive Material	Light?
	1st							
	2nd							
	3rd							
	4th							

3. Rename Sheet2 "3–4," and then label column A "Action to Light a Bulb," column B "Attempt," column E "Action to Make a Flashlight," and column F "Order." Merge cells H1 and I1 and label the merged cells "Attempts."
4. Create a list in cells A2 through A9 with the following items (figure 4.8; see "Lists via Data Validation" in the appendix):
   a. Connect wire to top of battery
   b. Connect wire to bottom of battery
   c. Connect 1 wire to one side of light bulb
   d. Connect other wire to other side of light bulb
   e. Connect both wires to one side of bulb
   f. Connect both wires to opposite side of bulb
   g. Connect both wires to top of battery
   h. Connect both wires to bottom of battery

FIGURE 4.8

ACTION TO LIGHT A BULB

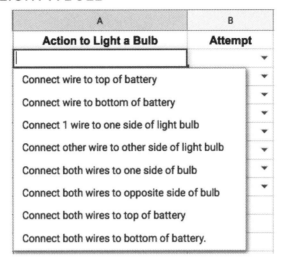

5. Create a list in cells B2 through B9 for Attempt 1 through Attempt 8 (see "Lists via Data Validation" in the appendix; figure 4.9).

FIGURE 4.9

ATTEMPT LIST

Action to Light a Bulb	Attempt
	Attempt 1
	Attempt 1
	Attempt 2
	Attempt 3
	Attempt 4
	Attempt 5
	Attempt 6
	Attempt 7
	Attempt 8

6. Create a list in cells E2 through E9 with the following (see "Lists via Data Validation" in the appendix):
   a. Connect light to 1 wire
   b. Connect light to 2 wire

     c. Connect 1 wire to battery top

     d. Connect 2 wire to battery bottom

     e. Tape battery to tube

     f. Tape light to tube

     g. Tape lens over end

7. Create a list in cells F2 through F9 with step 1 through step 7 (see "Lists via Data Validation" in the appendix).

8. In column H, select cells H2 through H9 and insert checkboxes in those cells (see "Insert a Checkbox" in the appendix).

Exploration

Kindergarten through Second Grade

During step 5 of the activity, learners test a variety of items to see which ones will allow electricity to pass through and light the bulb and which ones will not. Ask learners to record material tested in column H. A yes or no should be placed in the corresponding row in column I. After testing all the available materials, demonstrate how to create an organizational chart of columns G and H (See "Organizational Chart" in the appendix). Ask learners if they see a pattern.

After conducting the activity, demonstrate how to take apart a flashlight and put it back together again. Ask learners to observe closely as you do this. Then instruct learners to move the image of the flashlight part to the row that indicates whether it goes back together in the first, second, third, or fourth step. Depending on how the images were added to the sheet (inside the cell or over the cell), they can be dragged to the appropriate cell or copied and pasted into the cell. Have learners test their order by using it to take the flashlight apart and then put it back together. Ask if that is the only order in which the flashlight could go back together. Have learners rearrange the items in the spreadsheet and test the resulting order with the flashlight.

Third and Fourth Grades

Before conducting the activity, show learners sheet 3–4 of the Google Sheet. Given the list of items in column A, ask learners which process will enable the light bulb to light. Share the Google Sheet with learners (individually or in groups) and instruct them to make a copy. Tell learners to select an action to light a bulb and attempt from the corresponding lists, starting with Attempt 1. Ask learners to try that action with the light and battery.

Instruct learners to repeat the process until they are successful. Ask them how many attempts it took them. Remind them that success is not defined by the number of attempts; more attempts demonstrate persistence, showing that the learner is not giving up.

During step 6 of the activity, while learners are putting together their flashlights, have them select an item from the list in column E and then label it with the step in column F. Then have learners test the flashlight with the materials. Ask them to keep track of their attempts in columns H and I. Remind them that persistence is important; it's more important to understand and learn than to get it right the first time.

Ask learners to graph their number of attempts by selecting columns H and I and then clicking on the Explore icon in the lower left corner (see "Explore Button" in the appendix). Ask individuals or groups to share their graphs with the class. What do all the graphs have in common? Most likely, all the graphs will show multiple attempts.

Fifth and Sixth Grades

Before completing the activity, share the link to the Google Sheet with learners individually or in groups. Repeat the third- and fourth-grade Exploration, but this time ask learners to note the successes with the checkboxes in column C. Ask learners how they might graph their number of attempts and their number of successes.

During step 8 of the activity, ask learners to modify their flashlights to include a switch so it can be turned on and off. Ask learners to think about a way to track their attempts and successes on the Google Sheet so they can be graphed. When learners are finished, have them share their graphs showing successes and attempts and ask what each graph has in common. Most likely, learners should see that all graphs show more attempts than successes. Ask learners how they tracked their tests and designs. Discuss the benefits of one tracking system over another.

Suggested Picture Books

The suggested picture books share the theme of lights and power, all at different levels of understanding. In *Lights Out,* a storm causes a power outage. In the first chapter of *Zap!,* a boy tries to make a circuit, but it doesn't work. In *The Magic School Bus and the Electric Field Trip*, Ms. Frizzle's class explores electricity and how it's made. Each book can be used with learners to provide background and context for building a flashlight.

....

Title: *Lights Out*
Author: Jacqueline Jules
Suggested Grade Levels: 1–2

Summary: A storm causes the power to go out in Sofia's home. She and her father go to the store for supplies and plan a fun evening with the lights out.

Conversation Starter:
  1. Use the Talk It Out or Write It Down questions, or both, on page 29 of the book.

Title: *Zap!*
Author: Martha Freeman
Suggested Grade Levels: 5–7

Summary: When the power goes out in his town, Luis decides to investigate what caused the shutdown.

Conversation Starters (based on chapter 1 of the book)

1. What did Luis do that he shouldn't have? Why shouldn't he have done that?
2. After doing the activity, ask, "Why do you think Luis's light bulb wouldn't light?" Remember he says he "followed directions looked up online to create a circuit—battery connected to wire connected to switch connected to bulb, then back to wire and battery."
3. Do you think Luis's circuit is a good science fair project? Why or why not?

Title: *The Magic School Bus and the Electric Field Trip*
Author: Joanna Cole
Suggested Grade Levels: 2–6

Summary: Ms. Frizzle takes the class on a field trip through the town's electric wires so they can learn how electricity is generated and how it is used.

Conversation Starters:

1. What is an electric current?
2. On page 12, Ralphie is using a magnet to make a needle move on a meter. Why won't the needle move?
3. Why did the school experience a blackout?
4. Fuel is used to heat steam. What does the steam do? How does it help generate electricity?
5. As a class, map out the steps used to make electricity in the power plant.
6. Make a list of all the items in the classroom that require electricity to run.

REFERENCES AND NONFICTION RESOURCES

Butterworth, C. 2017. *How Does My Home Work?* Somerville, MA: Candlewick Press.

Deane-Pratt, A. 2011. *Electrical Gadgets.* New York, NY: PowerKids Press.

Nydal Dahl, Ø. 2016. *Electronics for Kids: Play with Simple Circuits and Experiment with Electricity!* San Francisco, CA: No Starch Press.

Parker, S. 2013. *Electricity.* New York, NY: DK Publishing.

BUILDING A RUBE GOLDBERG MACHINE ENGINEERING CHALLENGE

Learners explore basic engineering principles and simple machines by building a three-step Rube Goldberg machine. Learners in kindergarten through second grade focus on push and pull. Learners in third and fourth grades and in fifth and sixth grades explore the six simple machines. Learners are encouraged to explore the engineering design process by experimenting with different ideas to determine what works best.

Essential Questions

- What are simple machines and how do they work?
- What are the steps of the engineering design process?

Science Background for Educators

Rube Goldberg was a Pulitzer Prize–winning cartoonist. Although he graduated from the University of California Berkeley with a degree in engineering, he spent the majority of his career as a cartoonist. In fact, it is estimated that he created more than fifty thousand cartoons in his lifetime. His cartoons often depicted zany and complicated inventions, involving many steps to perform a simple operation—in other words, a chain-reaction machine.

Rube Goldberg machines use a variety of simple machines chained together in a complex way to perform a simple operation. There are six kinds of simple machines: wheel and axle, pulley, wedge, screw, gear, and lever.

1. *Wheel and Axle.* An axle is a rod that runs through a wheel. When the axle is turned, the wheel also turns and vice versa. You can see this action in a skateboard or a handcart (figure 4.10).

FIGURE 4.10

AXLE AND WHEELS

2. *Pulley.* A pulley uses a rope and a wheel to pull a heavy object. The rope is looped over the wheel. One end of the rope is attached to the load. The rope is pulled up or down to lift or lower the load (figure 4.11).

FIGURE 4.11

PULLEY AND WEIGHT

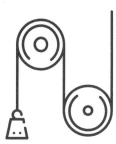

3. *Wedge.* A wedge can be used to split things. It typically has a sharp, pointed edge. When lowered, it can cause an object to crack open. An axe is a type of wedge (figure 4.12).

FIGURE 4.12

AXE

4. *Screw.* A screw has a spiral pattern that allows it to be inserted into other materials when rotated. The screw holds things together with a downward force (figure 4.13).

FIGURE 4.13

SCREW

5. *Gear.* A gear is wheel that has teeth on the outer rim. When one gear is pushed against another, both gears turn (figure 4.14).

FIGURE 4.14

GEARS

6. *Lever.* A lever is a bar that rests on a point called a fulcrum. When you push on one end of the lever, the other end lifts. This action helps lift heavy objects (figure 4.15).

FIGURE 4.15

LEVER AND FULCRUM

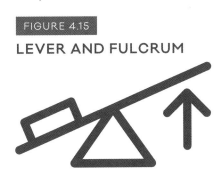

★ **COLLABORATION TIP**

Learners will naturally be able to create more complex Rube Goldberg machines the more they understand and have experience with each type of simple machine. Classroom educators and school librarians can work together to explore the different types of simple machines over the course of several weeks. After gaining basic exposure to a Rube Goldberg machine, learners can make pulleys, explore levers, build cogs, and so on in the school library. At the end of their introductions to these concepts, they can make a more complex Rube Goldberg machine in the classroom with the school librarian's help and then showcase their completed creations in the school library for other learners, educators, administrators, and parents to see.

National Standards

Grade Level	AASL Standards Framework for Learners	Next Generation Science Standards: Science and Engineering Practices	National Core Arts Anchor Standards
K–2	I.A.1. Learners display curiosity and initiative by formulating questions about a personal interest or a curricular topic. V.B.1. Learners construct new knowledge by problem solving through cycles of design, implementation, and reflection. III.C.1. Learners work productively with others to solve problems by soliciting and responding to feedback from others. V.D.3. Learners develop through experience and reflection by open-mindedly accepting feedback for positive and constructive growth.	**Practice 3. Planning and Carrying Out Investigations** • With guidance, plan and conduct an investigation in collaboration with peers (for K). **Practice 4. Analyzing and Interpreting Data** • Analyze data from tests of an object or tool to determine if it works as intended.	Anchor Standard 2. Organize and develop artistic ideas and work. Anchor Standard 5. Develop and refine artistic techniques and work for presentation.
3–4		**Practice 1. Asking Questions and Defining Problems** • Define a simple design problem that can be solved through the development of an object, tool, process, or system and includes several criteria for success and constraints on materials, time, or cost.	
5–6			

Materials

- Things that roll (e.g., marbles, balls, toy cars)
- Things that move (e.g., mousetrap, dominoes, fan)
- Things that can serve as a ramp (e.g., toy train tracks, marble runs, books, PVC pipe, plastic tubing)
- Containers (e.g., cardboard boxes, plastic water bottles, cans)
- Other household materials (e.g., aluminum foil, popsicle sticks, rulers, wooden blocks, bowls, string, tape, sand, water)

Activity

 THINK

1. Explain the six types of simple machines (see "Science Background for Educators") and show learners images of each type of machine. Explain that learners will watch a video with lots of simple machines in it. You want learners to see if they can find each type of machine in the video.
2. Explain who Rube Goldberg was and how his ideas came about (see "Science Background for Educators"). Show learners a video of a Rube Goldberg machine. The band OK Go made a video called *This Too Shall Pass* that is currently available

on YouTube. It depicts a very complex Rube Goldberg machine that cannot be replicated in the classroom, but the video will be fun to watch and will give learners an idea of what a Rube Goldberg machine consists of and how it works.

3. Ask kindergarten through second-grade learners to name their favorite part of the machine. What was happening? Lead them to the terms *push* and *pull*. What was being pushed? What was pulled? Ask third- and fourth-grade and fifth- and sixth-grade learners to call out each type of simple machine they see or pause the video periodically to quiz them on the type of simple machine in use.

4. Explain that the people who build machines, both simple and complex, are called *engineers*. The first step in the engineering design process is to determine the problem that needs solving. Ask learners to think about simple problems that could be solved with a machine, such as ringing a bell or shutting a door. As a class, decide on a task to try.

 CREATE

5. Explain that the next step in the engineering design process is to use your imagination to come up with a plan based on what you know and what you find out as you try new things. Explain that engineers often have to try things lots of times before they get it right. The important thing is to learn from failure. What went wrong? How do I fix it?

6. Form groups of learners and explain that each group will build a three-step Rube Goldberg machine that will do the decided-upon task.

7. Provide groups with a variety of materials.

 GROWTH MINDSET TIP

As learners create and test different setups, they will likely fail a few times. Remind learners that failure is part of the design process. We learn from our mistakes and discover how things really work.

---

8. Remind kindergarten through second-grade learners to think about how they can push or pull things. Do they need to push or pull harder? In a different direction? Using a different object? Remind third- and fourth-grade and fifth- and sixth-grade learners to think about the six types of simple machines and how each could be used to accomplish the task.

 SHARE AND GROW

9. Explain that engineers typically work together. They share ideas and learn from each other. Have each group share its Rube Goldberg machine. Groups can share with each other if there is not enough time for everyone to share with the whole class.

10. Ask learners why something did or didn't work. If it didn't work, how could they fix it or try again? If it did work, what else could they use to do the same thing?
11. If time allows, ask learners to share their suggestions for improvement and ask the groups to try the suggestions.

Assessment

Ask third- and fourth-grade learners what types of simple machines they used in their Rube Goldberg machines. Ask all learners why something did or didn't work. If it didn't work, how could they fix it or try again? If it did work, what else could they use to do the same thing?

Technology Integration

Learners use Google Sheets to plan and revise their Rube Goldberg machines before building.

Before Exploration

1. Create a new Google Sheet (see "Create a New Sheet" in the appendix).
2. Title columns A through E "Step," "Action," "Push or Pull," "Machine Type," and "Object."
3. In cells C2 through C5, build a list with two options: push and pull (see "Lists via Data Validation" in the appendix).
4. In cells D2 through D5, build a list with six options: wheel and axle, pulley, wedge, screw, lever, and gear (see "Lists via Data Validation" in the appendix).
5. In cells E2 through E5, build a list of all the materials you collected for use in building the Rube Goldberg machines (e.g., book, doorstop, string, marble, etc.).

Exploration

Kindergarten through Second Grade

After step 6 of the activity, review the materials that learners have available to use in building their Rube Goldberg machine. Share the Google Sheet with learners and demonstrate how they should choose an item from the Object column and then in column C indicate whether the item should push or pull. After learners have picked objects, instruct them to decide how the objects will be used by either drawing or writing the action in the Action column.

During step 8 of the activity, as learners are building and testing their machines, remind them that if a design does not work, they can try different materials. However, they should be sure to change their responses on the Google Sheet to match their redesign.

After the activity, ask learners how much they referred to the design on their Google Sheet while building. How much did they change the design? If this were a big project, like making a car, would the Google Sheet be helpful? Why or why not?

Third and Fourth Grades

Repeat the kindergarten through second-grade Exploration, but this time ask learners to copy and paste their three steps before editing so there is a record of each design iteration (figure 4.16).

FIGURE 4.16

GRADES 3–4 SPREADSHEET

fx					
	A	**B**	**C**	**D**	**E**
1	Step	Action	Push or Pull	Machine Type	Object
2	1	pluck	pull ▼	pulley ▼	rubber band
3	2	roll	push ▼	wedge ▼	marble
4	3	hit	push ▼	lever ▼	domino
5					
6	1	pluck	pull ▼	pulley ▼	rubber band
7	2	roll	push ▼	wedge ▼	marble
8	3	roll	push ▼	wheel and axle ▼	toy car

After the activity, ask learners how many times they had to redesign. Ask how they referred to the Google Sheet to guide what they were building. Did the Google Sheet help learners agree on what to build before beginning? Why or why not? If this were a large project like building a car, how would the Google Sheet be helpful?

Fifth and Sixth Grades

Repeat the third- and fourth-grade Exploration; however, during step 9 of the activity, allow learners to view each other's Google Sheets. Learners can use the comment feature to provide feedback to other groups and make notes on features they see in other groups' designs that they would like to try. If time allows, ask learners to make one more round of revisions based on their classmates' feedback.

Suggested Picture Books

The following picture books present stories on the themes of engineering, inventions, and the design process. Each book features a character who comes up with an idea that fails, but each character perseveres to refine and retest until the invention works. *Ben Franklin's Big Splash: The Mostly True Story of His First Invention* depicts Ben Franklin's process in inventing a set of water fins for swimming. In *Rosie Revere, Engineer,* Rosie is ashamed by all her inventions that have failed, but her aunt shows her how having a flop is different than failing. Izzy Gizmo finds a crow with a broken wing and decides to invent a new wing for the crow, but her first few attempts don't quite work. In the first chapter of *Ellie, Engineer,* Ellie decides to build a water balloon launcher, but she can't do it on her own.

....

Title: *Ben Franklin's Big Splash: The Mostly True Story of His First Invention*
Author: Barb Rosenstock
Suggested Grade Levels: K–3

Summary: The story of young Ben Franklin and his first invention: how he started with a question, came up with an idea, tested a prototype, and improved it until it worked.

Conversation Starters:
1. What process did Ben go through to swim more like a fish?
2. What question did Ben first ask himself that led to the development of his swim fins?
3. Have you ever used or seen swim fins? How do they differ from Ben's? How are they the same?

....

Title: *Rosie Revere, Engineer*
Author: Andrea Beaty
Suggested Grade Levels: K–2

Summary: Rosie Revere likes to take odds and ends and create great inventions, but she's afraid to share them with the world, until a visit with her aunt shows her that having a flop isn't the same as failing.

Conversation Starters:
1. Why was Rosie afraid to share her inventions?
2. What does Rosie say the only true failure is?
3. What sort of things would you like to invent?

Title: *Izzy Gizmo*
Author: Pip Jones
Suggested Grade Levels: K–2

Summary: Izzy loves inventing new things, but her inventions don't always work and she often gives up. When she finds a crow with a broken wing, she tries to help, but nothing is working. What will she do?

Conversation Starters:
1. Why did Izzy give up when her Swirly-Spagsonic, Tea-Mendous, and Beard-Tastic all broke?
2. What problem was Izzy trying to solve when she was inventing wings for the crow?
3. Was Izzy able to fix the crow in one try? How did she improve her design over time?

Title: *Ellie, Engineer*
Author: Jackson Pearce
Suggested Grade Levels: 2–4

Summary: Ellie loves to invent things. She decides to build a doghouse and needs help, but first she needs to get everyone to work together.

Conversation Starters (based on chapter 1 of the book; read only the first chapter because the entire book is 166 pages long):
1. What problem was Ellie trying to solve with her water balloon launcher?
2. Why do you think the balloon launcher threw the balloons farther than Ellie could on her own?
3. Is Ellie allowed to use electric tools without her parents watching? Why?

REFERENCES AND NONFICTION RESOURCES

How to Be an Engineer. 2018. New York, NY: DK Publishing.

"Who Was Rube Goldberg?" 2018. *Rube Goldberg.* https://www.rubegoldberg.com/rube-the-artist/.

DESIGNING A THERMOS
EXPLORING HEAT

Learners will perform an experiment to test what makes the best insulator by making a thermos using paper cups, aluminum foil, and various filler materials (e.g., water, foil, cotton balls, shredded paper, straw, sand, etc.). In the kindergarten through second-grade activity and the third- and fourth-grade activity, learners work as a class or in groups, with each group of learners making a thermos with a different material and then comparing their results. Fifth- and sixth-grade learners will design their own experiment to test for a single variable.

Essential Questions
- What is an insulator?
- What materials make the best insulators?

Science Background for Educators

Heat and temperature are not the same. Heat describes the transfer of thermal energy between molecules within a system. Heat measures how energy moves or flows. Temperature, on the other hand, describes the average kinetic energy of molecules within a system. Another way to think of the difference is the fact that heat is a measure of change and temperature is a measure of the property of a material.

The warmer a material, the faster the molecules move. When hotter (faster) molecules bump into colder (slower) molecules, they transfer some of their energy. This is how heat flows from warm objects to cooler ones. Insulation slows this process. Most insulation has lots of air spaces, because the air creates space between the molecules, resulting in less bumping and, therefore, less heat transfer.

Materials
- Electric hot water heater
- Paper cups in two sizes so that one will fit inside the other with space between the two (figure 4.17)

FIGURE 4.17

PAPER CUP PLACED INSIDE ANOTHER

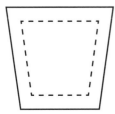

National Standards

Grade Level	AASL Standards Framework for Learners	Next Generation Science Standards: Science and Engineering Practices	National Core Arts Anchor Standards
K–2	I.A.2. Learners display curiosity and initiative by recalling prior and background knowledge as context for new meaning. I.B.1. Learners engage with new knowledge by following a process that includes using evidence to investigate questions. II.C.2. Learners exhibit empathy with and tolerance for diverse ideas by contributing to discussions in which multiple viewpoints on a topic are expressed.	**Practice 3. Planning and Carrying Out Investigations** • With guidance, plan and conduct an investigation in collaboration with peers (for K). • Make observations (firsthand or from media) and/or measurements to collect data that can be used to make comparisons.	Anchor Standard 11. Relate artistic ideas and works with societal, cultural and historical context to deepen understanding.
3–4	I.D.3. Learners participate in an ongoing inquiry-based process by enacting new understanding through real-world connections.	**Practice 3. Planning and Carrying Out Investigations** • Plan and conduct an investigation collaboratively to produce data to serve as the basis for evidence, using fair tests in which variables are controlled and the number of trials considered.	
5–6	I.A.2. Learners display curiosity and initiative by recalling prior and background knowledge as context for new meaning. II.C.2. Learners exhibit empathy with and tolerance for diverse ideas by contributing to discussions in which multiple viewpoints on a topic are expressed. V.C.2. Learners engage with the learning community by co-constructing innovative means of investigation. I.D.3. Learners participate in an ongoing inquiry-based process by enacting new understanding through real-world connections.		

- Aluminum foil
- Various materials that can be used for insulation (e.g., cotton balls, shredded paper, water, straw, sand, foil)

Activity

 THINK

1. Remind learners about the story of the three bears and how each bowl of porridge was a different temperature. Ask learners to brainstorm reasons for the different temperatures. Guide learners to the idea that the container the porridge is in might affect how fast it cools off.
2. Explain that a material that keeps something from changing temperature is called an *insulator*. An insulator can keep warm things warm and cool things cool. Ask learners to name some insulators they are familiar with (e.g., coat, mittens, hat, thermos, cooler, etc.).
3. Show learners a cup of hot water. Explain that they are going to use homemade materials to make a thermos to keep the water warm as long as possible.
4. Ask learners to name different reasons why someone might choose one thermos over another (e.g., price, size, heat retention, design).

 CREATE

5. Explain that learners will make a thermos out of the materials available and determine which materials make the most effective thermos. Show learners the materials they have to choose from and ask them to predict which material is the best insulator.
6. Explain that in order to make this a true experiment, there can be only one variable; otherwise, it would be hard to tell what was causing the difference between each test. Therefore, everything should be the same for each test except the insulator itself.
7. Kindergarten through second-grade learners can build one thermos for each material to be tested. Form groups of learners and have each group make a thermos with a different type of insulator, or have the whole class build all the thermoses and assign roles to learners so that everyone has something to do (e.g., cup handler, insulator handler for each type of insulation, thermometer reader, data recorder, etc.).
8. With third- and fourth-grade and fifth- and sixth-grade learners, explain that each group will get two cups (one large and one small) and a bit of aluminum foil. Each group will also get one of the insulating materials. Every group will make a thermos that is exactly the same except for the material inside.
9. For kindergarten through second-grade and third- and fourth-grade learners, model how to make the thermos by adding a little insulation to the bottom of

the large cup, placing the small cup inside the large one (see figure 4.17), then filling the space between the two cups with more of the same insulative material (figure 4.18). Tip: If you have more time, have learners work together to design the thermos first, rather than giving them instructions on how to build one.

FIGURE 4.18

THERMOS EXPERIMENT SETUP

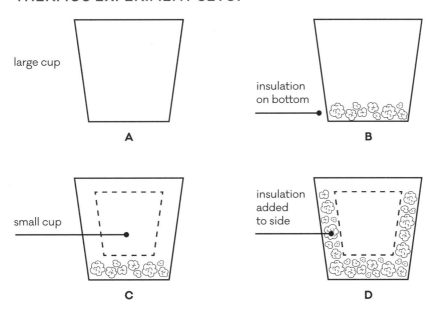

10. Form groups of fifth- and sixth-grade learners and ask each group to design an experiment to test the insulative value of each material. As groups successfully design an experiment, ask them to share with groups that are struggling.
11. Distribute materials as needed. When learners have made their thermoses, ask them to predict which material will be the most effective insulator and explain why they think so. Fill each small cup with hot water and have learners cover their cups with foil. When all cups are filled, ask each group to put a thermometer in their cup (poke it through the foil), measure the temperature of the water, and write it down. Safety Tip: Learners should be careful not to spill the hot water.
12. Set a timer for ten minutes. After ten minutes, have each group measure the temperature of the water again and calculate the difference.
13. During the ten-minute waiting period, show learners two identical transparent bowls or cups. Add cold water to one container and very hot water to the other. Add a drop of food coloring to each container and ask learners to observe what happens over the next one to two minutes. In which container did the food coloring spread faster?

14. Explain that everything in the world is composed of atoms and molecules. When atoms and molecules move, they create heat. The faster they move, the more heat they create. We can't see the heat directly, but we can feel it, and we can see how it affects the world around us.

 SHARE

15. After ten minutes, ask each group to share the material it tested and the temperature change. Record the results on the board.
16. Which insulator was the most effective? Were learners' predictions correct? Why or why not?

 GROW

17. If time allows after cleaning up, ask learners to stand. Ask them to recall how the food coloring moved in the containers (the food coloring in the hot water moved faster). Remind learners that molecules move faster the warmer they are. Ask learners to move their bodies to model how cool molecules move. What about hot molecules? Warm molecules?

Assessment

Ask learners to draw a picture of a thermos that is a good insulator and label their drawing. Encourage learners to draw the thermos they would like to use if they could (color, design, etc.) as well as one that is a good insulator. Do learners' drawings indicate an understanding of what makes a good insulator?

Technology Integration

Learners will evaluate thermos designs by collecting and graphing the temperature of each thermos.

Before Exploration

1. Create a new Google Sheet (see "Create a New Sheet" in the appendix).
2. In row 1, merge cells A and B and label the merged cell "Cup A." Repeat this pattern of merging two cells for each material you wish to test and label the resulting merged cells "Cup B," "Cup C," and so on.
3. In row 2, add the headings "Time" and "Temperature" in the two cells under each Cup label.
4. In each Time column, enter "0" and "10" (figure 4.19).

FIGURE 4.19

THERMOS TEMPERATURE SPREADSHEET

fx						
	A	**B**	**C**	**D**	**E**	**F**
1	**Cup A**		**Cup B**		**Cup C**	
2	**Time**	**Temperature**	**Time**	**Temperature**	**Time**	**Temperature**
3	O	212	O	212	O	212
4	5	190	5	200	5	200
5	10	175	10	190	10	180
6	15	150	15	185	15	180
7	20	100	20	180	20	175
8	30	80	30	175	30	170

Exploration

Kindergarten through Second Grade

After learners have built their thermoses in step 11 of the activity, show them how to measure the temperature of each cup and enter it in the Temperature columns of the Google Sheet. If time allows, modify the activity so that learners measure the temperature every five minutes for up to thirty minutes. Modify the Google Sheet accordingly.

After learners have measured the temperature, demonstrate how to graph the data using the line chart (see "Line Chart" in the appendix). Point out that the x-axis represents time, the y-axis represents temperature, and each line represents a different cup. Ask learners which material was the better insulator (held heat the longest). Ask learners to use evidence from the graph to prove their answer.

Third and Fourth Grades

Repeat the kindergarten through second-grade Exploration; however, provide learners a shareable link and ask them to make a copy and record data on their own Google Sheet (see "Sharing Sheets" in the appendix). Also, when graphing the data, encourage learners to try different graphs (see "Choosing and Setting Up Charts" in the appendix). Which type of chart displays the data in a way that makes the most sense and that helps them understand how the temperature has changed?

Fifth and Sixth Grades

Repeat the third- and fourth-grade Exploration, but this time help learners create their own Google Sheet and label it with the appropriate headings based on the experiment they design during the activity. After the Exploration, ask groups to compare their Google Sheets. Did they all design their data collection tool the same? Is one design more effective than another? Why might that be the case?

Suggested Picture Book

The picture book featured in this activity addresses the theme of insulation. *The Magic School Bus in the Arctic: A Book about Heat* includes a section on using snow as an insulator.

....

Title: *The Magic School Bus in the Arctic: A Book about Heat*

Author: Joanna Cole

Suggested Grade Levels: K–6

Summary: Ms. Frizzle takes the class to the Arctic to explore heat and insulation.

Conversation Starters:

1. What objects in the book kept things warm? (Examples include paper in jackets, polar bear fur, seal fat, etc.)
2. What is an insulator?
3. What makes snow an insulator?

REFERENCES AND NONFICTION RESOURCES

Walker, S. M. 2005. *Heat*. Minneapolis, MN: Lerner.

READY TO RECYCLE
TRASH-TO-TREASURE CHALLENGE

After a brief introduction to the concepts of reusing and recycling, learners will be given "trash" and asked to design something using the "trash," tape, scissors, and other common items. Kindergarten through second-grade learners will be given free exploration time to make a "new" object from reused materials. Third- and fourth-grade learners will be challenged to make the strongest structure they can using recycled and reused materials. Fifth- and sixth-grade learners will be challenged to use the "trash" to build a tool that can complete a task.

Essential Questions
- How can trash be recycled or reused?
- How do the characteristics of a material determine what it can be used for?

Science Background for Educators

For thousands of years, trash was mostly tossed into the street. In 1280, London, England, instituted a rule prohibiting people from tossing trash out the window, but because there was nowhere else to put the trash, people largely ignored the prohibition. All the trash in the streets attracted cats, dogs, mice, bugs, and the like that ate the trash and carried diseases such as the bubonic plague, which resulted in the deaths of one-third of Europe's population between 1347 and 1352.

In 1912, England came up with a "new" way to deal with trash. Residents dug a pit, put the garbage in it, compacted it, and then covered it with dirt. The dirt helped prevent the trash from blowing away and mitigated the stench. This pit became known as a sanitary landfill, and landfills are still in use.

Some things we throw away are biodegradable. This term means that those things are eaten by microorganisms in the soil. Over many years, the materials are broken down by the microorganisms, and all their nutrients are returned to the soil. Anything that was part of a living thing is biodegradable, such as a bone, a potato peel, feces, a plant, and so on. As microorganisms break down biodegradable materials, they produce methane. In the natural environment, typically small amounts of methane are produced in a small area, and they are dispersed throughout the air in the soil. However, when trash is put in a landfill, it is compacted. Compacting the trash helps reduce the amount of space it takes up, but it also reduces the oxygen present in the soil. Therefore, the methane builds up quickly. Methane is a flammable gas, so in many landfills, pipes are used to move the gas out of the trash so it can be burned in a controlled way. When methane is burned, it produces carbon dioxide, which contributes to climate change.

The other problem caused by landfills is the sludge that collects at the bottom of the pit. Although landfill operators do their best to keep everything dry, some water filters into the garbage. As it passes through the trash, the water picks up chemicals and then pools up at the bottom. A thick barrier, called a *leachate*, is placed to prevent this contaminated water from leaching into the soil below the landfill and getting into groundwater, but barriers can leak, and the leachate itself can cause health problems.

Communities that don't use landfills sometimes burn their trash. This burning can cause toxic gases to be released into the air. Some communities, such as in Sweden, have harnessed this gas and used it to generate electricity. However, the ash that is produced still contains the toxic chemicals that were in the garbage and must be disposed of somewhere.

Many communities gather up plastics, paper goods, aluminum, glass, and other materials and recycle them. These materials are broken down in large factories so they can be remade into new products.

With creative thinking, however, we can reuse things that people typically think of as trash. Food waste can become compost. Old clothes can be sewn into new clothes or used as insulation. Old plastic bottles can be filled with dirt or trash and used as building materials. Around the world, people are coming up with creative ways to transform garbage into new things.

> ★ **COLLABORATION TIP**
> Learners will not have sufficient time to engage in the full design process. Classroom educators can use this beginning exploration of reusable and recyclable materials as a starting point for a more complete design process. Learners can continue to refine and test their designs in the classroom. Additionally, this activity would be an ideal start or end to a collaborative recycling unit. The school librarian can guide learners to appropriate resources and teach them how to engage ethically with those resources to find and communicate information about waste and recycling.

Materials
- Scissors
- Tape
- Glue
- Toilet paper tubes (4)
- Filling material (e.g., popcorn, gravel, sand, cotton, etc.)
- Plastic wrap

National Standards

Grade Level	AASL Standards Framework for Learners	Next Generation Science Standards: Science and Engineering Practices	National Core Arts Anchor Standards
K–2	V.A.2. Learners develop and satisfy personal curiosity by reflecting and questioning assumptions and possible misconceptions. V.B.2. Learners construct new knowledge by persisting through self-directed pursuits by tinkering and making. I.C.1. Learners adapt, communicate, and exchange learning products with others in a cycle that includes interacting with content presented by others. V.D.2. Learners develop through experience and reflection by recognizing capabilities and skills that can be developed, improved, and expanded.	**Practice 6. Constructing Explanations and Designing Solutions** • Use tools and/or materials to design and/or build a device that solves a specific problem or a solution to a specific problem. **Practice 8. Obtaining, Evaluating, and Communicating Information** • Communicate information or design ideas and/or solutions with others in oral and/or written forms using models, drawings, writing, or numbers that provide detail about scientific ideas, practices, and/or design ideas.	Anchor Standard 1. Generate and conceptualize artistic ideas and work. Anchor Standard 11. Relate artistic ideas and works with societal, cultural and historical context to deepen understanding.
3–4	V.A.2. Learners develop and satisfy personal curiosity by reflecting and questioning assumptions and possible misconceptions. V.B.1. Learners construct new knowledge by problem solving through cycles of design, implementation, and reflection. V.B.2. Learners construct new knowledge by persisting through self-directed pursuits by tinkering and making.	**Practice 3. Planning and Carrying Out Investigations** • Make observations and/or measurements to produce data to serve as the basis for evidence for an explanation of a phenomenon or test a design solution. **Practice 6. Constructing Explanations and Designing Solutions** • Generate and compare multiple solutions to a problem based on how well they meet the criteria and constraints of the design solution.	
5–6	I.C.1. Learners adapt, communicate, and exchange learning products with others in a cycle that includes interacting with content presented by others. V.C.3. Learners engage with the learning community by collaboratively identifying innovative solutions to a challenge or problem. V.D.2. Learners develop through experience and reflection by recognizing capabilities and skills that can be developed, improved, and expanded.	**Practice 6. Constructing Explanations and Designing Solutions** • Undertake a design project, engaging in the design cycle, to construct and/or implement a solution that meets specific design criteria and constraints. • Apply scientific ideas or principles to design, construct, and/or test a design of an object, tool, process or system. **Practice 7. Engaging in Argument from Evidence** • Evaluate competing design solutions based on jointly developed and agreed-upon design criteria.	

- Decorating tools (e.g., colored paper, markers, crayons, etc.)
- "Trash" (e.g., cardboard tubes, empty boxes, aluminum cans, plastic bottles, old books/catalogs, etc.)
- Small weights (nuts and bolts can be used)

Preparation

Fill three toilet paper tubes, each with a different material (gravel, cotton, sand, etc.). Leave one tube empty. Using plastic wrap and tape, cover both ends of the filled tubes to secure the filling.

Activity

 THINK

1. Ask third- and fourth-grade learners what their school building is made of (wood, concrete, bricks, etc.). Are some materials stronger than others? How would they know? Show them the four toilet paper tubes. Explain that each one is filled with a different material. Together, learners are going to test which material is the strongest. Ask learners if they have any ideas about how to test for strength. If learners are having difficulty coming up with an answer, guide them to the idea of stepping on each material and measuring the change in height. The stronger material will not collapse as much. As a class, perform the experiment that learners develop.

2. Show all learners the "trash" items that you have collected for this activity. Ask learners what they see. Ask them how these items are used. Ask learners to think of other ways they could use these items.

3. Briefly share the story from *The Soda Bottle School*. If you have time, read the book. Otherwise, share how the residents of a town in Guatemala had two problems—their school was too small, and they had a lot of plastic bottles that were going in the trash. To solve both these problems, the townspeople built their school out of plastic bottles. First, because plastic bottles are not very strong on their own, residents filled the bottles with trash and dirt. Next, they put chicken wire on the frame of the building and then they made a wall of the filled bottles one row at a time, tying the bottles to the chicken wire. Finally, they coated the outside of the bottle wall with cement so the bottles were hidden. Amazing what people can do when they think creatively!

 CREATE

4. Explain that learners will be challenged to make something "new" with the trash. Kindergarten through second-grade learners can make whatever they want with the time and materials they have. Third- and fourth-grade learners

should make a structure that will be tested to see how much weight it can hold. Fifth- and sixth-grade learners should make a tool; their tool can do anything the learners want, such as pick up an object, open a door, or flip a switch.

 ### SHARE AND GROW

5. Ask each learner or group of learners to demonstrate what they created and how they made it. What challenges did they encounter? Test the strength of third- and fourth-grade learners' structures by placing a paper cup on top and adding one weight at a time until the structure tips or collapses. Ask third- and fourth-grade learners to think about what they could change to make their structure stronger next time. Ask fifth- and sixth-grade learners what they would try to make their tool more effective. What did each group learn from the successes or failures of their group or the other groups?
6. Ask learners to think about the things they throw away at home. How could they reuse some of those items? What about some of the items they throw away at school?

 GROWTH MINDSET TIP

Remind learners that growth sometimes involves changing our behaviors. Ask learners to think about things they didn't used to do that now they do, such as helping around the house, making their own lunch, cleaning their room, and so on. Encourage learners to be proud of the changes they've made to improve themselves.

Assessment

Take photos of learners with their work. On a sheet of paper, have learners write the name of the item they made and what it's made of. Put learners' photos and trash-to-treasure descriptions on display.

Technology Integration

Learners collect and graph data from their trash-to-treasure activity based on type, amount, and effectiveness.

Before Exploration

1. Create a new Google Sheet (see "Create a New Sheet" in the appendix).
2. Add three new sheets to the Google Sheet and label them "K–2," "3–4," and "5–6" (see "Adding Sheets" in the appendix).

3. On sheet K–2, add the headings "Objects" to cell A1, "Most Used" to cell B1, "Unused" to cell C1, and "Total Number" to cell D1.
4. In the "Objects" column, type the items available for learner design so there is one item in each cell.
5. On sheet 3–4, add the headings "Primary Material" to cell A1 and "Weight (lbs)" to cell B1.
6. On sheet 5-6, add the headings "Trials" to cell A1 and "Effectiveness" to cell B1.

Exploration

Kindergarten through Second Grade

After the activity, call out each item from column A on sheet K–2 and ask learners to show with their fingers how many of that item they used in their design. Add up learner responses and record them in column B. Do this for each item. Ask learners to help count how many items were not used (i.e., are still left in the supply pile) and record these data in column C.

Demonstrate how to add columns B and C using the SUM equation (see "Equations" in the appendix). Graph the data using a column chart (see "Column Chart or Bar Chart" in the appendix). Ask learners if they were able to use most of the materials available. Which materials were easiest to reuse? How does the graph provide evidence for their conclusions?

Third and Fourth Grades

After step 5 of the activity, help each group of learners record their primary building material in column A of sheet 3–4 and the maximum weight their structure could hold in column B. Graph the class data using a column chart (see "Column Chart or Bar Chart" in the appendix) and discuss the resulting graph. Which material is strongest? How does the graph provide evidence to support learners' conclusions?

Fifth and Sixth Grades

After completing the activity, provide a shareable link to the Google Sheet and help learners make a copy. Explain that the Google Sheet will be used to allow them to collect data on the effectiveness of their tool so they can redesign and retest it. Decide on a scale for effectiveness (e.g., 1 = very effective, 5 = not at all effective).

Demonstrate how to record the trial number (1, 2, 3, etc.) in column A and the effectiveness scale number in column B. Instruct learners to redesign and retest their prototype, recording the new trial in row 2. Learners should repeat this process at least four times.

Demonstrate how to graph the resulting data and ask learners to share with the class. Discuss how collecting and graphing the data were useful or not and why.

What did groups learn from testing four different versions of their prototype? Were they able to improve their prototype each time? If not, what did they learn from the exercise?

Suggested Picture Books

The suggested picture books tell true stories of how reusing and recycling materials helped solve problems. In *The Soda Bottle School,* a community in Guatemala got rid of its plastic bottles and expanded its school at the same time by using the plastic bottles in the construction of a new building. In *One Plastic Bag,* Isatou Ceesay and a group of women in Gambia make new products from plastic bags that are polluting their community.

Title: *The Soda Bottle School*
Author: Laura Kutner
Suggested Grade Levels: K–4

Summary: In the village of Granados, Guatemala, the school was running out of room. Then one person got an idea that led to the perfect solution.

Conversation Starters:
1. What was the problem with Fernando's school?
2. What is an *ecoladrillo*? Why is it stronger than an empty bottle?
3. How long did it take Fernando and his town to collect all the bottles they needed? How many bottles did they need?
4. What did the builders use to hold the bottles upright? What else do you think could have been used?
5. Were the bottles visible when the builders were done? Why or why not?

Title: *One Plastic Bag: Isatou Ceesay and the Recycling Women of the Gambia*
Author: Miranda Paul
Suggested Grade Levels: 2–6

Summary: In Gambia, plastic bags were thrown away and began to form large heaps in the streets. They were collection spots for water, which brought mosquitos and disease. Livestock tried to eat them and were killed. Isatou Ceesay found a way to recycle the bags and transform her community.

Conversation Starters:

1. What problems were being caused by the plastic bags?
2. Why did the women have to crochet in the candlelight, away from others?
3. What items in your home do you throw away that you could reuse or recycle?
4. What else do you think could be done with a plastic bag?

REFERENCES AND NONFICTION RESOURCES

Fyvie, E. 2018. *Trash Revolution: Breaking the Waste Cycle.* Toronto, ON: Kids Can Press.

Mulder, M. 2015. *Trash Talk: Moving toward a Zero-Waste World.* Victoria, BC: Orca Book Publishers.

Pratt, M. 2015. *How Can We Reduce Household Waste?* Minneapolis, MN: Lerner.

BOBBING BOATS
FLOATING AND SINKING

Learners will explore why things float or sink by building boats. After a demonstration, kindergarten through second-grade learners will test how much weight is needed to make a submarine—a container that doesn't float or sink but hovers in the water. Learners in third and fourth grades and in fifth and sixth grades will apply the principles of air volume and density to build self-righting boats using the available materials.

Essential Questions
- What is density?
- What is the relationship between density and whether something floats or sinks?

Science Background for Educators

Whether or not something floats is a matter not of its weight but of its density. Density can be calculated as mass divided by volume. The density of water is 1 gram per cubic centimeter. Things that have a lower density than water will float in water, and things with a higher density will sink.

When something is floating in water, it displaces the water. The water that is being displaced pushes back with an upward force. This force is called *buoyancy*. Archimedes (287–212 BC) discovered that an object will displace the same amount of water as the object's volume. For example, if the volume of a stone is 3 grams, it will displace 3 grams of water. Items that float also displace water, but they will displace only an amount equal to the portion of the object that is under the water. For example, a ball floating in water displaces only a small amount of water, not the entire volume of the ball. Archimedes also realized that the water pushes back against a floating or sinking object. In fact, the object will sink until its weight is equaled by the upward force of the water.

> ★ **COLLABORATION TIP**
>
> Exploring buoyancy can involve a great deal of math. After learners explore buoyancy in these introductory activities in the school library, the classroom educator can build on the lesson by introducing measurement. In the lower grades, learners can measure the weight they are using in their boats. Older learners can measure the density of various objects by calculating the air volume and the weight to determine which objects are most likely to float and which will sink.

National Standards

Grade Level	AASL Standards Framework for Learners	Next Generation Science Standards: Science and Engineering Practices	National Core Arts Anchor Standards
K–2	I.A.2. Learners display curiosity and initiative by recalling prior and background knowledge as context for new meaning. I.B.1. Learners engage with new knowledge by following a process that includes using evidence to investigate questions.	**Practice 3. Planning and Carrying Out Investigations** • Evaluate different ways of observing and/or measuring a phenomenon to determine which way can answer a question. • Make observations (firsthand or from media) and/or measurements to collect data that can be used to make comparisons.	Anchor Standard 10. Synthesize and relate knowledge and personal experiences to make art.
3–4	I.C.2. Learners adapt, communicate, and exchange learning products with others in a cycle that includes providing constructive feedback. V.D.3. Learners develop through experience and reflection by open-mindedly accepting feedback for positive and constructive growth.	**Practice 3. Planning and Carrying Out Investigations** • Make observations and/or measurements to produce data to serve as the basis for evidence for an explanation of a phenomenon or test a design solution.	
5–6		**Practice 3. Planning and Carrying Out Investigations** • Collect data to produce data to serve as the basis for evidence to answer scientific questions or test design solutions under a range of conditions.	

Materials
- Oranges (2 per class)
- Aluminum foil
- Tape
- Plastic bottles (1 per group)
- Tubs
- Water
- Flat lids (large and small)
- Miscellaneous items to add weight to the boat (e.g., rice, putty, etc.)
- Miscellaneous items to build boats (e.g., cardboard, plastic food trays, etc.)
- Scale (for Technology Integration)

Activity

 THINK

1. Fill a bowl with water. Ask all learners to predict what will happen when you put an orange in the bowl of water. Place the orange in the bowl and ask learners to observe what happens. Retrieve the orange and peel it. Ask learners what they think will happen when you put the peeled orange in the water. Place the peeled orange in the water.

2. Ask learners if they can guess why the unpeeled orange floated and the peeled orange did not. Explain that the skin of the orange has air in it. This air helps keep the orange afloat in the water. When the skin is removed, the air pockets are removed, and now the orange will sink. The peel is like a life jacket for the orange—it is filled with air and helps keep the orange afloat.

3. Introduce the word *density*. Explain that whether an object sinks or floats depends on its density. If the object is denser than the water, it will sink; if it is less dense, it will float. An unpeeled orange is less dense than water, so it floats. A peeled orange is denser than water and so it does not float.

4. Explain to third- and fourth-grade learners that the air inside the hull of a boat is like the air in a life jacket or an orange peel. It helps keep the boat afloat. Demonstrate by placing a ball of aluminum foil in the water. Then fold another sheet of foil of the same size into the shape of a boat and put that on the water.

5. Show fifth- and sixth-grade learners a tub of water, two flat lids, and some weights. Place the small lid on the water and stack the weights on it until it sinks. Ask learners to predict whether the large lid will sink with less, more, or the same amount of weight. Ask learners to justify their predictions. Put the same amount of weight on the large lid. Explain that the greater surface area of the large lid allows it to hold more weight and still float. This feature is called *surface tension* and plays a role in why things float or sink.

6. Explain to fifth- and sixth-grade learners that another thing that influences whether something floats or sinks is the amount of air it contains. The amount of air in an object affects its density, and density affects whether something floats or sinks. Objects that have a greater density than water will sink in water, and objects with a lower density will float. Demonstrate by crushing a piece of foil into a loose ball. Place the foil ball in the water; it should float. Then tighten the ball and return it to the water; it should sink. Explain that both objects have the same amount of foil and the same weight, but the looser ball is less dense because it has more air.

 CREATE

7. Form groups of kindergarten through second-grade learners and give each group an empty plastic bottle and a tub of water. Instruct groups to create a submarine (an object that doesn't sink to the bottom and doesn't float on the top, but

hovers under the water). Learners should experiment by adding rice or other material to the bottle to see whether it will float or sink or hover. As learners are experimenting, ask them what strategies they are using. Are they adding all the rice or other material at once and then removing some? Adding a little at a time? Starting with a random amount and then adding or reducing?

8. Explain to third- and fourth-grade learners that one of the challenges engineers encounter is ensuring that their boat will not tip over. Form groups of learners and challenge them to design a boat that will stay upright. Provide each group with an empty bottle and a tub of water to test in. Provide access to the other materials, such as rice, aluminum foil, putty, and tape. As learners are designing, ask them questions about their choices, such as, "What do you think will happen if you . . . ?" and "Why did you choose to . . . ?"

9. Form groups of fifth- and sixth-grade learners and challenge them to use the available materials to design a boat that will hold the greatest amount of weight before sinking. Each group can be given a tub of water, or one tub of water can be used by all groups to test their boats when they are ready. Ask learners how they will test to see which boat can hold the most weight. As learners are designing, ask them questions about their choices, such as, "What do you think will happen if you . . . ?" and "Why did you choose to . . . ?" Encourage learners to remember the demonstrations at the beginning of the activity.

 SHARE AND GROW

10. Ask learners to compare their results. Did all groups get similar results? Discuss why or why not. Ask kindergarten through second-grade groups to share the strategies they used to find the right amount of rice or other material to make their vessel into a submarine. Ask third- and fourth-grade learners to share their designs with the class and then test their boats.

11. Describe to third- and fourth-grade learners how boats stay upright by using ballast, typically heavy sand that weights the bottom of the ship to prevent it from rolling over. As a class, discuss which boat performed best and why.

12. With fifth- and sixth-grade learners, discuss which boat performed best and why. Ask learners what they would do differently next time to build a better boat. What did they learn from each other's designs?

 GROWTH MINDSET TIP

Encourage learners to think about the comparison between each group's creation as an opportunity to learn from each other, not as a means of ranking anyone's ability, talent, or intelligence.

Assessment

Ask kindergarten through second-grade learners to determine when the density of their submarine was greater than, less than, or equal to the density of water. When it was floating? Sunk? Hovering under the water?

Ask third- and fourth-grade and fifth- and sixth-grade learners what they would do differently next time to build a better boat. What did they learn from each other's designs? Do third- and fourth-grade learners' explanations and discussion reflect an understanding of density or ballast, or both? Do fifth- and sixth-grade learners' boat design choices reflect an understanding of surface tension?

Technology Integration

Learners collect data in Google Sheets about the materials used to fill their plastic bottles to explore volume and density.

Before Exploration

1. Create a new Google Sheet (see "Create a New Sheet" in the appendix).
2. Create two new sheets and label the three sheets "K–2," "3–4," and "5–6" (see "Adding Sheets" in the appendix).
3. On sheet K–2, label cell A1 "Inside the Bottle," cell B1 "Float or Sink," cell C1 "Material Added," and cell D1 "Depth in Water."
4. On sheet 3–4, label cell A1 "Boat," cell B1 "Weight," and cell C1 "Float Scale."
5. On sheet 5–6, label cells A1 to E1 "Material Added (g)," "Volume (mL)," "Density," "Float or Sink," and "Water = 1 g/mL."
6. For the kindergarten through second-grade plastic bottles, hold a ruler parallel to the plastic bottle. Using a Sharpie, mark a 1/centimeter scale onto the side of the bottle, starting with 0 at the base and increasing the numbers toward the top (figure 4.20).

FIGURE 4.20

PLASTIC BOTTLE
WITH CENTIMETER
SCALE

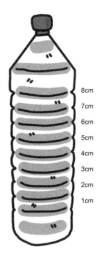

Exploration

Kindergarten through Second Grade

During step 7, assign roles within the groups. One learner should be responsible for measuring the material to be recorded in column C of sheet K–2. Material can be measured with a weight-based scale or by reading the scale on the side of the bottle. One learner should be responsible for reading the scale on the side of the bottle when the bottle is in the water to ascertain its depth in the water. Depending on group size, a learner can be responsible for recording what is inside the bottle (e.g., air; water; rice or other material; one-half air and one-half water; one-half rice or other material and one-half air; etc.) and whether the bottle floats or sinks. This recording also can be done by the whole group. However, one learner should be responsible for entering the data into the Google Sheet or reporting the data to the school librarian to be recorded.

After learners have recorded their data, demonstrate how to select columns B, C, and D and click the Explore button to generate a graph (see "Explore Button" in the appendix). Ask learners to choose a graph that best represents what is happening in this experiment and why. Discuss their choices.

Third and Fourth Grades

Share the Google Sheet with each group and show learners how to navigate to sheet 3–4. Designate one learner in each group to record the data into the Google Sheet. As learners are testing their designs, they should record the design number (1, 2, 3, etc.) in column A, indicate in column B how much weight the boat could hold before tipping, and record in column C how far it sank based on the scale on the side of the bottle.

When learners are done testing and collecting data, ask them to select columns B and C and graph them as a line chart (see "Line Chart" in the appendix). Show learners how to make column B the x-axis and column C the y-axis. Learners may wish to explore different graphs to explain how weight affected whether the boat tipped or floated upright. Ask learners if they see any pattern in the data as they compare all the groups' graphs and data sets.

Fifth and Sixth Grades

During step 9 of the activity, share the Google Sheet with learners and demonstrate how to select sheet 5–6. Demonstrate how to measure the volume of rice or other material in the cylinder. Demonstrate how to measure the weight of rice or other material in the bottle (measure the bottle while empty, measure the bottle with rice or other material added, then subtract the two values). Show learners how to enter the equation for Density (density = mass / volume) in column D by typing "=B1/C1" in cell D1 and then copying the equation to the rest of column D (see "Equations" and "Copying and Pasting Text" in the appendix). Add a "1" to cell E1 and copy down the rest of column E.

Guide learners to compare the density of their bottle (column D) with the density of water (column E) to guess whether it will float or sink before testing it in the tub of water.

Suggested Picture Books

The suggested picture books expose learners to the ideas of density, floating, and sinking. In *Who Sank the Boat?* a variety of animals join each other on a boat. Each time another animal climbs aboard, it seems like the boat will sink. *What Floats in a Moat?* explores the idea of ballast as two characters attempt to float barrels of buttermilk across a moat. Ms. Frizzle's class explores surface tension in Scholastic's *The Magic School Bus: Ups and Downs—A Book about Floating and Sinking. Things That Float and Things That Don't* presents an introduction to buoyancy for any learner.

Title: *Who Sank the Boat?*
Author: Pamela Allen
Suggested Grade Levels: K–1

Summary: A cow, donkey, sheep, pig, and mouse decide to go for a row in a boat, but the boat doesn't get very far. Who sank the boat?

Conversation Starters:
1. The mouse is the smallest animal, but he caused the boat to sink. Why do you think that is?
2. The cow almost sank the boat when he stepped in. What could he have done to avoid tipping the boat?

Title: *What Floats in a Moat?*
Author: Lynne Berry
Suggested Grade Levels: K–3

Summary: Archie the Goat and Skinny the Hen experiment with trying to cross a moat.

Conversation Starters:
1. Why would the barrel full of buttermilk not float?
2. Why did the empty barrel float but tip over?
3. What do you think ballast is? How do you think it works?

Title: *Scholastic's The Magic School Bus:*
Ups and Downs—A Book about Floating and Sinking
Author: Jane Mason
Suggested Grade Levels: 2-6

Summary: Ms. Frizzle's class hears about a monster in the lake and wants to investigate, but how will they get to the bottom? And once there, how do they get back up?

Conversation Starters:
1. What did Ms. Frizzle's class do to cause the boat to sink?
2. How did Ms. Frizzle describe the force of the water that causes the boat to go back to the surface?
3. Why did crumpling the piece of bread make it sink when a regular slice of bread did not? What was different about the bread?
4. How did the class get the boat to stay at the bottom of the lake?

Title: *Things That Float and Things That Don't*
Author: David A. Adler
Suggested Grade Levels: 2-4

Summary: This introduction to density and how it affects buoyancy is presented in an easy-to-understand manner.

Conversation Starters:
1. What is density?
2. What has a lower density than water?
3. Why does a lump of clay sink, but clay shaped into a boat floats?
4. Is the density of ice more or less than the density of water? Why?

REFERENCES AND NONFICTION RESOURCES

Farndon, J. 2003. *Buoyancy*. Tarrytown, NY: Marshall Cavendish.

CODING WITH CUPS
DESIGNING A STRUCTURE USING CODE

Learners in kindergarten through second grade will work in pairs to create a two-dimensional design out of small cups based on a simple arrow-based code; learners then test their code by asking another pair of learners to re-create their design. Learners in third and fourth grades will build on this idea by adding the coding idea of loops. In fifth and sixth grades, learners will explore "if statements" in addition to basic code and loops.

Essential Questions
- What is computer code?
- What is an algorithm?
- How do computers understand various instructions?

Science Background for Educators
We are surrounded by computer programs. Many of the machines we use have computers in them that use programs to tell them what to do. Computers, cell phones, televisions, newer vehicles, washing machines, and more all use computers to function. Coding is the act of writing the code that the computers use to execute their programming.

Some basic terminology is helpful for understanding computer coding:
- An *algorithm* is a set of instructions that tells a computer what to do, like the set of steps in a recipe. Computers use algorithms to complete a variety of tasks.
- The *sequence* is the order of steps the algorithm goes through to perform the task. It's important that steps be in the correct sequence.
- *Code* is the language computers use to understand algorithms. Algorithms are written in code.
- Sometimes computers need to repeat a task. Instructions that specify repeating something over and over are called *loops*.
- *If statements* or *if-then-else statements* are decisions computers make based on certain conditions.

★ **COLLABORATION TIP**

This short introduction to coding does not involve technology. School librarians and other educators can build on this initial understanding of code and algorithms by having learners explore coding for real using tools such as Scratch (https://scratch.mit.edu/) to write stories or design games. There are numerous books and online lesson plans for using Scratch in the classroom. In either the school library or the classroom, learners can design a simple story or game on paper; in the other space, they can translate that idea into computer code. At the conclusion of the unit, learners can host a computer story/game event in the school library to showcase their programs for their families and other learners.

National Standards

Grade Level	AASL Standards Framework for Learners	Next Generation Science Standards: Science and Engineering Practices	National Core Arts Anchor Standards
K–2	V.A.2. Learners develop and satisfy personal curiosity by reflecting and questioning assumptions and possible misconceptions. V.B.1. Learners construct new knowledge by problem solving through cycles of design, implementation, and reflection. V.D.1. Learners develop through experience and reflection by iteratively responding to challenges.	**Practice 2. Developing and Using Models** • Develop and/or use a model to represent amounts, relationships, relative scales (bigger, smaller), and/or patterns in the natural and designed world(s). **Practice 5. Using Mathematics and Computational Thinking** • Use counting and numbers to identify and describe patterns in the natural and designed world(s).	Anchor Standard 1. Generate and conceptualize artistic ideas and work.
3–4 5–6		**Practice 2. Developing and Using Models** • Use a model to test cause and effect relationships or interactions concerning the functioning of a natural or designed system. **Practice 5. Using Mathematics and Computational Thinking** • Create and/or use graphs and/or charts generated from simple algorithms to compare alternative solutions to an engineering problem.	Anchor Standard 1. Generate and conceptualize artistic ideas and work. Anchor Standard 3. Refine and complete artistic work.

Materials

- Small cups (5–10 per pair of learners)
- Grid (1 per pair of learners; draw a grid on a sheet of blank paper such that each square is slightly larger than the diameter of the top of a cup [figure 4.21])
- Graph paper (or blank paper; graph paper makes it easier for learners to write their code because they can put one instruction in each square, but blank paper works fine too)

FIGURE 4.21

CUP ON GRID

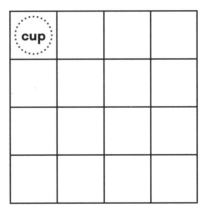

Activity

 THINK

1. Explain to all learners that an algorithm is a set of instructions a computer uses to complete a task. Any set of steps can be considered an algorithm. People use algorithms to complete everyday tasks, just like computers. Draw or write an algorithm on the board to illustrate this concept. For example, an algorithm of brushing your teeth might look like this:

    a. Take lid off toothpaste tube.

    b. Pick up toothbrush.

    c. Wet toothbrush.

    d. Put toothpaste on toothbrush.

    e. Brush teeth.

    f. Spit out toothpaste.

    g. Rinse toothbrush.

    h. Put toothbrush back in holder.

    i. Put lid on toothpaste.

2. Explain that learners are going to play a game using an algorithm. Ask for two volunteers: one volunteer will be the computer engineer giving instructions to the computer, and the other volunteer will be the computer. Have the "engineer" stand with her back to the "computer" so she can't see what the "computer" is drawing. Explain that the engineer should provide instructions to the computer on how to draw a smiley face. Instruct the other learners in the class to stay quiet and not coach or provide additional directions.

3. As a class, discuss how hard it can be to give good directions. Talk about the importance of being specific, being precise, and providing a good order of steps. Does the circle for the face come first? Or the two dots for the eyes? Or the mouth?

 CREATE

4. Form pairs of learners. Explain that each pair will receive a grid, a set of small paper cups, and a blank sheet of graph paper. Pairs will use the cups to build a two-dimensional structure (meaning the cups should all be on the surface of the table, not stacked). Then each pair of learners will write an algorithm that another pair of learners will use to re-create the cup arrangement. Instead of using words, however, learners will use arrow symbols.

5. Demonstrate by building a pyramid shape with four cups (figure 4.22). Show learners how to write the directions for building this shape using arrows and symbols. Explain that computers don't read and write like we do; rather, they use what's called *code*. For this activity, the code will consist of arrows and symbols. The arrows describe the direction of movement across the grid, and the symbols indicate whether to pick up or drop a cup. Remind learners that computers don't guess or make assumptions; they won't automatically assume that they need to go back to the starting square to pick up another cup.

FIGURE 4.22

CODING CUPS EXAMPLE

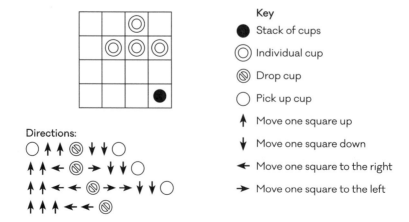

6. Provide each pair with supplies (cups, grid, and a blank sheet of graph paper). Give learners five minutes to come up with a design and then sufficient time to write the code (directions) for how to re-create the design.

7. Explain to third- and fourth-grade and fifth- and sixth-grade learners that sometimes we need computers to do a task over and over. Instead of writing the instructions again and again and again, engineers write a loop. If learners have a cup that moves up three times, instead of saying "move up move up move up," they can say "move up X3" to show that this step should be done three times. Ask learners to rewrite their code using loops.

 SHARE

8. When learners are done writing their code, ask them to re-stack their cups and trade directions with another pair of learners. Explain that having someone else test your code is a typical part of the computer programming process. Can each pair re-create the pattern the other learners came up with?

 GROW

9. Introduce the concept of an if statement to fifth- and sixth-grade learners. Explain that sometimes we want computers to do something only if a particular condition is met. For example, perhaps you are creating a game and you want your character to dress for the weather. You would tell the character to wear sunglasses if it's sunny, carry an umbrella if it's raining, and wear a hat and gloves if it's snowing. Explain that learners will play a short "if statements game." Ask each learner to write an if statement for their classmates, such as, "If you have brown hair, hop three times." Have learners take turns reading their if statements for the other learners to follow. Are there any statements that no one could follow? Remind learners that when something isn't right in a piece of code, the error is called a *bug*. Can they debug any nonworking if statements so that they work?

10. Explain to all learners that when something isn't right in a piece of code, the error is called a *bug*. Engineers do an action called *debugging* when they fix those pieces of the code. People can make mistakes, but computers can only do what the code tells them to do. If a computer doesn't do what we want, it's because the code has a bug and needs to be debugged.

11. Discuss what worked and what didn't. Was there a problem with the code? Was there a step missing? Or in the wrong order? Was there a problem with following the directions?

12. If time allows, have learners try to debug their code or the code of another pair of learners or write a new piece of code that accomplishes the same pattern with a different set of steps.

Assessment

During the Share step, did learners write a good algorithm that was easy for other learners to follow? Did third- and fourth-grade learners successfully convert their code into one containing loops in step 7? As learners are discussing in step 11, prompt them to use the vocabulary they have just learned (*code, algorithm, bug*). Do they use those terms correctly?

Technology Integration

Learners use a Google Sheet to practice the step-by-step process of writing and debugging a program.

Before Exploration

1. Create a new Google Sheet (see "Create a New Sheet" in the appendix). You may want to have a different sheet for each grade level (see "Adding Sheets" in the appendix) or create a new Google Sheet for each grade level.
2. In row 1, enter "Left," "Right," "Up," and "Down" starting at cell A1. In row 2, add a picture of an arrow matching the word above it using Insert > Image (see "Insert an Image" in the appendix). In cells A3 and B3, add the headings "Algorithm" and "Debug."
3. Generate a shareable link to share with learners or link on a class website.

Exploration

Kindergarten through Second Grade

After learners are done writing their code on their paper in step 6 of the activity, ask them to open the Google Sheet and make a copy. Explain to learners that they will use the letter to represent the symbol based on the key in rows 1 and 2. Ask them to transfer their paper instructions to the sheet. When they are done, have learners "run" the program by building it with their cups or give their program to another pair of learners to re-create as in step 8 of the activity. When learners encounter an error that prevents them from placing their cups correctly on their grid, have them type the word *Error* in column B next to the cell where the error occurred (figure 4.23).

After pairs of learners have tested their code, show them how to copy and paste the sequence into column C, correct the error by editing the cell where the error occurred, and repeat the process until the program runs smoothly.

Ask learners if they think this process is similar to problem solving when designing software. How about when solving math problems?

FIGURE 4.23

K–2 CODE EXAMPLE

fx				
	A	**B**	**C**	**D**
1	l=left	r=Right	u=Up	d=Down
2	←	→	↑	↓
3	Alogrithm	Debug		
4	l		l	
5	r		r	
6	l		l	
7	u	Error	d	
8	u		u	
9	r		r	
10	r		r	
11	l		l	
12	u		u	

Third and Fourth Grades

Repeat the kindergarten through second-grade Exploration, but before asking learners to debug their program, ask them what they need to do on the Google Sheet if they want to include a loop. Show learners how to use Autofill to replicate their loop (see "Autofill" in the appendix). Show learners how to test and debug their code (see the kindergarten through second-grade Exploration).

Ask learners if it is a good idea to debug before or after adding loops. Why or why not?

Fifth and Sixth Grades

Repeat the third- and fourth-grade Exploration, but this time ask learners to use conditional formatting to color their cells based on the letter in the cell (see "Conditional Formatting" in the appendix). Ask learners if they can see a color pattern where their loop exists. Could they change their code so there is a color pattern, and would the code still work?

Suggested Picture Books

These suggested picture books address introductory principles associated with coding. In *How to Code a Sandcastle,* a girl and her robot use coding concepts to build a sandcastle, while overcoming various challenges. The selected chapter in *Spotlight on Coding Club!* portrays a group of girls deciding what type of app to create and how they will go about the app creation process. *Grace Hopper: Queen of Computer Code* is a biography of a legendary computer coder who worked for the U.S. Navy.

Title: *How to Code a Sandcastle*
Author: Josh Funk
Suggested Grade Levels: K–2

Summary: Pearl uses her robot friend Pascal to build a sandcastle using fundamental computer coding concepts such as sequences and loops.

Conversation Starters:
1. How did Pearl change her instructions for Pascal so he would find the best place to build a sandcastle?
2. What is a loop? How did Pearl use one to make her job easier?
3. How did Pearl use if-then-else to solve her problem?
4. Did Pearl give up when high tide washed away her castle? How did she overcome that challenge?

Title: *Spotlight on Coding Club!*
Author: Michelle Schusterman
Suggested Grade Levels: 4–6

Summary: The talent show is coming up and the coding club has been asked to make the web app that learners will use to submit their video entries and place their votes.

Conversation Starters (based on chapter 1 of the book)
1. What is feature creep? How did it impact the girls' choices regarding the app they were designing?
2. What did the girls do first after deciding to work on the voting feature of the app?
3. Why is brainstorming helpful? What does it help you to do?

Title: *Grace Hopper: Queen of Computer Code*
Author: Laurie Wallmark
Suggested Grade Levels: K–6

Summary: This is the story of Grace Hopper, who revolutionized computer coding.

Conversation Starters:
1. Why are computer glitches called *bugs*?
2. Why did Grace rig a clock to run backward? How did the clock help her?
3. How old was Grace when she retired from the Navy the second time?

REFERENCES AND NONFICTION RESOURCES

Di Lernia, G. 2017. *DK Findout! Coding.* New York, NY: Dorling Kindersley.

Lyons, H., and E. Tweedale. 2016. *Coding, Bugs, and Fixes.* Minneapolis, MN: Lerner.

PART III

Making STEAM Work for You

CHAPTER 5

Writing Your Own Scaffolded Lesson Plans

lementary-age children naturally express themselves through art. Learners are prone to expressing their interest through drawing, coloring, making clay models, and more. As a result, incorporation of the arts into STEM concepts is a simple way to engage learners' knowledge of these topics.

Once you've decided to write a STEAM lesson plan, there is no one right or wrong approach. Many lesson plan and curriculum models have been created by researchers and professional organizations. If you have one that works for you, use it!

However, if you need some ideas, you can follow the approach that was taken in this book: write an essential question, determine the learning task, write the learning plan, scaffold the plan, and revise the plan as needed.

BEGIN WITH AN ESSENTIAL QUESTION

Each lesson begins by identifying an essential question. In other words, what should learners understand at the conclusion of the lesson? For example, in the "Fast Surfaces: Experimenting with Friction" activity, the intent is for learners to understand the nature of friction and how friction can vary between different surfaces. In the same vein, you could start with a standard from the *National School Library Standards,* the Next Generation Science Standards, or the National Core Arts Standards as the goal. The *National School Library Standards* crosswalk with the Next Generation Science Standards is a particularly useful tool for this purpose. Once you have identified a Shared Foundation and a Domain or Competency from the *National School Library Standards* that you wish to address with learners, use the crosswalk to locate a science and engineering practice that is aligned with your chosen Shared Foundation and Domain or Competency within a particular grade level. For example, if you wish to address the Competency "Learners engage with new knowledge by following a process that includes using evidence to investigate questions" (AASL 2018, Learner I.B.1.) with third-grade learners, you might use the crosswalk to identify the following science and engineering practice: "Make a claim about the merit of a solution to a problem by citing relevant evidence about how it meets the criteria and constraints of the problem" (NGSS Practice 7: Engaging in Argument from Evidence). Although this science and engineering practice can be used with any STEAM activity, the crosswalk identifies that within the NGSS, it is aligned to the performance expectation 3-LS4-4. The crosswalk helps facilitate opportunities to collaborate with a classroom or science educator.

It's important to keep in mind that whether you use an essential question or a standard as the starting point for your lesson, learners will never fully master a concept in one lesson. Mastery requires repeated practice over time and in different contexts, and most standards and essential questions are complex and challenging.

DETERMINE THE LEARNING TASK

After writing the essential question, it's important to determine the learning task. What will learners do to demonstrate that they understand the essential question? Although this assessment can technically be accomplished with a worksheet or quiz, learners will be more engaged and have a greater opportunity to develop skills associated with the *National School Library Standards* and the Next Generation Science Standards if an inquiry-based approach is taken. For this book, lessons are sorted into two categories: those that ask learners to think like a scientist and those that ask learners to design like an engineer. If the activity asks learners to think like a scientist, the learning task involves a scientific investigation. Learners may be asked to design or conduct an experiment or do both, make observations, collect or analyze data or do both, and so on. For example, in "Making a Tissue Box Guitar: Exploring Sound," learners conduct a simple experiment using different types of rubber bands to explore vibration. If the activity asks learners to design like an engineer, the learning task involves designing or building an object or tool (or doing both) using design principles, such as in "Bobbing Boats: Floating and Sinking," in which learners design a boat that is self-righting.

WRITE THE LEARNING PLAN

The next step of the lesson plan is the learning plan itself—the steps the school librarian or classroom educator and the learner will go through during the lesson or activity. At this stage, choose one grade level or grade band to write for and compose a lesson plan for that group of learners. You will scaffold the activity later. As you write, make sure learners are engaging in inquiry-based or project-based learning. Give them an opportunity to ask questions, try new things, and challenge themselves rather than giving them questions for which the answers are already known or for which there is only one right answer.

As you write, consider using the Think (cognitive), Create (psychomotor), Share (affective), and Grow (developmental) Domains from the *National School Library Standards* to provide structure to the activities and ensure that learners have an opportunity to practice Competencies in a purposeful way. For example, in "Ready to Recycle: Trash-to-Treasure Challenge," learners begin in Think by questioning assumptions and misconceptions when they contemplate how items that we typically perceive as trash can be used in new and different ways (AASL 2018, Learner V.A.2.). Then, in Create, they work through cycles of design as they are challenged to create something "new" with the trash (AASL 2018, Learner V.B.1.). In Share and Grow, learners share their products with each other (AASL 2018, Learner I.C.1.) and then recognize capabilities and skills that can be developed, improved, and expanded (AASL 2018, Learner V.D.2.) when they identify items in their home that they can repurpose.

SCAFFOLD THE PLAN FOR YOUR LEARNERS

Once you've written the lesson or activity for one grade level or grade band, you can scaffold that activity up or down for the other grade levels or grade bands. For older learners, activities should be made more complex so that learners are asked to explore more advanced concepts, engage in more precise designs, or consider more elements in their design. For example, in "Working Together: Build-a-Tower Challenge," kindergarten through second-grade learners build a tower, whereas third- and fourth-grade learners are asked to build a tower that can withstand an earthquake, complicating the factors learners need to consider in their construction. The fifth- and sixth-grade learners are also asked to build a tower that can withstand an earthquake, but in addition they must take a budget into consideration. In this way, each grade level is working on the same concept with the same (or very similar) materials but with greater complexity.

REMAIN OPEN TO REVISING THE PLAN

Finally, the lesson plan or activity can be revised to include additional elements based on school and school library programmatic needs. In this book, there is a focus on developing a growth mindset. Therefore, tips on how to help learners shift toward a growth mindset are included in each activity. Even when writing for yourself, tips like these can help you draw out those specific elements so they do not get lost or minimized during the activity.

As you write and revise your own STEAM lesson plan, you might also consider these possibilities for differentiation or extensions in your plan or for scaffolding of your plan:

1. Begin with a book that introduces learners to the necessary vocabulary of the content area. During, or after, reading the book, help learners generate a list of the new words they have learned and practice those words before engaging in the new content. The book will help engage learners' curiosity, and the vocabulary will increase learners' confidence in the subject matter.

2. While reading the related books, engage learners with critical thinking questions that encourage them to make connections across disciplines and to their own experience.

3. Utilize the expertise in your building. If you have a music or art educator in your school, seek that person's advice about the design of your lesson or ask the individual to help co-teach—or do both. Also seek the help of any educators in your building who are particularly interested, or well trained, in a STEAM field.

4. Look for opportunities to collaborate with other educators and to have learners collaborate with each other. Giving learners the opportunity to work with others in a different grade level can help them develop social skills while meeting learning objectives.

No matter what approach you take to lesson planning, developing a scaffolded STEAM lesson plan will allow you to differentiate learning in a way that is more manageable. Find inspiration wherever you can. As you see activity ideas in other books, in blog posts, or shared by your fellow educators, consider writing a scaffolded version. If your lesson doesn't quite work the first time, remember the growth mindset strategies you are attempting to instill in your learners, make modifications, and try again.

CHAPTER 6

Strategies for Collaboration

When educators work together, they share knowledge and resources to directly and indirectly improve learners' growth. Collaboration between educators in the school community significantly impacts learners' academic achievement (e.g., Goddard, Goddard, and Tschannen-Moran 2007; Leana and Pil 2006; Ronfeldt, Farmer, McQueen, and Grissom 2015) and improves educator self-efficacy and job satisfaction (OECD 2014).

Nevertheless, the quality of collaboration varies across and within schools. Changing priorities, increasing demands on educators' time, lack of training, and insufficient time to collaborate can hinder even the most willing participant. When it comes to educator and school librarian collaboration in particular, school librarians report that collaboration "does not happen often enough, and the collaboration that does take place many times does not approach a level where the school library media specialist would be considered an indispensable member of the instructional team" (Cooper and Bray 2011, 48).

Many approaches can be found in the literature concerning how to bolster collaborative relationships and increase collaborative opportunities between school librarians and other educators and between educators in general. One of the most necessary steps to building collegial relationships is to establish and maintain trust. Trust between educators, and between educators and administrators, is so critical to effective collaboration that the level of trust among educators was the distinguishing characteristic between schools in Chicago that thrived under reform and those that did not (Bryk and Schneider 2003).

Improving instructional practice requires the acknowledgment of problems and areas of improvement. In trusting environments, educators are more likely to disclose more accurate, relevant, and complete information regarding problems. However, when distrust is present, especially when one individual holds more power within the organization, communication becomes an effort to protect one's personal interest rather than presenting accurate information and sharing ideas. To build this necessary trust, educators can adopt several strategies, outlined in the following sections.

DEMONSTRATE YOURSELF AS AN EXPERT

Whether you are a school librarian, a STEM educator, an art educator, a fifth-grade educator, or something else, demonstrate yourself as an expert in your specific content area. This approach may involve communicating the roles and responsibilities of your position to the other educators in the building. It is not uncommon for people to hold misconceptions about the job duties and responsibilities of others. We make decisions regarding whom to work with based on what we know and perceive, so misconceptions can definitely hinder those efforts. For example, if a classroom educator doesn't know that the school librarian can arrange for materials to be sent from another school, that educator will not know to work with the school librarian toward that goal.

COMMUNICATE CLEARLY AND CONSISTENTLY

When communication is frequent and clear, people gain a better assessment of each other's abilities, intentions, and likely behavior (Cross and Parker 2004). Connections should be present and strong in order to be most effective (Abrams, Cross, Lesser, and Levin 2003), meaning that intersections should include both a personal and a professional component. In other words, it's important to catch up on a personal level before engaging in work-related dialogue. Of course, not every encounter needs to follow this format, but it is important that the relationship as a whole include both parts for the most effective development of trust. Communication might consist of announcements and news, ideas about how to utilize resources, lesson ideas or specific resources targeted to a specific educator or group of educators, training opportunities, and examples of successful collaborations.

EXPRESS FIDELITY BETWEEN WORDS AND ACTIONS

If someone promises to do something and then does not, or does something else, it is likely that others will question that person's dedication to the community's interests. This situation is more complicated than it appears on the surface, however, especially in the busy environment of a school. In addition to words matching deeds, expectations must match deeds. This is why when a school librarian collaborates with another educator, it is important to lay out expectations. Who will accomplish what task and in what timeline? If expectations are not made explicitly, they might be assumed. Then, when they are not met, distrust can form.

To avoid a negative outcome, be explicit about expectations, be sure to stay organized, divide up tasks explicitly, and be realistic about your time commitments and abilities. Once those expectations are clearly set down, it is important they be enacted to build and maintain trust. This practice is particularly important when working with a new colleague or one with whom you haven't previously worked; a colleague who has a negative first impression has a much harder time gaining traction.

COLLABORATE STRATEGICALLY

Identify the key players in your school community. Which educators are perceived as leaders and trendsetters? These are the individuals you want to work with because they have influence with others in the community and can help create a bridge to other educators. If you are already a key player in the community, seek to build connections with those on the periphery who are not as involved or seem disconnected from the rest of the community. Collaboration with these individuals can help connect them to the greater school network and build a more effective team.

COME TO THE TABLE WITH AN IDEA

Sometimes the best approach is to come to the table with an idea in mind, as opposed to identifying an educator to work with first. If you approach the fifth-grade classroom educator with an idea that aligns to that individual's standards and priorities, the educator will be much more likely to work with you than if you come with no specific ideas. Using the *National School Library Standards* crosswalk with the Next Generation Science Standards is a great way to find a point of connection. The crosswalk can be used to find science and engineering practices or NGSS performance expectations that align with the *National School Library Standards.* These alignments can be used as a starting point for a collaborative lesson or unit.

Of course, another educator may wish to modify your idea, or your ideas may not be feasible at that point in time; either way, it is a good starting point for the conversation. Because each set of activities in this book presents a starting point for an investigation, use them as opportunities to collaborate with various educators. Within each activity, you'll see a collaboration tip with ideas for extending the learning in collaboration with another educator.

Regardless of how it is accomplished, when educators work together, they increase their knowledge base and resource pool to directly and indirectly benefit their learners.

CHAPTER 7

Assessing Learners' Work

I t can be difficult to fit in assessment in a thirty-minute class period. Nevertheless, it is important to check for learners' understanding. Within each activity in the book is an Assessment section with ideas for facilitating assessment. Carlson, Humphrey, and Reinhardt (2003) use the phrase *continuous assessment* to describe the type of assessment used in this book—assessment that occurs during inquiry investigations and through regular observations, rather than at the end of a unit. Continuous assessment is not meant to occur all the time but should be woven into the instruction such that it becomes almost indistinguishable from the learning itself.

This type of formative assessment does not need to be complex or difficult, but it should be tied to the essential question or a specific standard from the *National School Library Standards* or the Next Generation Science Standards. For example, in "Making a Tissue Box Guitar: Exploring Sound," one of the essential questions is "How does frequency impact pitch?" The assessment suggests that educators listen for learners' explanations of what is happening as they pluck the rubber bands on the "guitar." Do learners' discussions and explanations reflect an understanding of frequency and pitch?

Formative assessment is also not about giving learners a score or grade, although that may sometimes be involved. The purpose instead is to engage in a cycle of feedback and improvement for both learner and educator. The data in a formative assessment are used by the educator to plan instruction for a specific learner or group of learners or to determine next steps in a unit to ensure that learners are learning. In contrast, summative assessment is conducted at the end of the unit or term to demonstrate learner growth over a specified period.

FORMATIVE ASSESSMENT

Formative assessment can be conducted in a variety of ways. The key to effectively determining learners' understanding of the inquiry process and STEAM content areas is to conduct assessments throughout the course of the project, not just at an end point. The following are some easy-to-implement examples of formative assessment.

Learner Observation

The simplest way to conduct formative assessment is to observe learners' investigations and discussions. Are research questions testable? Can learners design a fair test for an experiment? Can they justify their explanations when discussing with peers? This observation may consist of listening and watching, or reviewing writing samples.

Exit Slips

An exit slip allows learners to reflect on what they have learned and express what they are thinking after exposure to new information. Exit slips can ask learners to document learning by writing one thing they learned today, emphasize the process of learning by sharing what they still have questions about, or even evaluate the instruction itself with such questions as these: "Did you enjoy working in small groups today? Why or why not?" Learners can write or draw their reflections.

Learners can state this information verbally or write the information on a small sheet of paper or electronically. There are advantages and disadvantages to each approach. Speaking aloud may offer an opportunity for discussion and clarification, but it may take more time and cannot be anonymous. Writing can be anonymous, or it can be identified but not shared with the rest of the class. This method provides learners a greater sense of comfort about sharing and increases the likelihood of an honest response. However, there is less opportunity for clarification of learners' responses, making it more difficult to make a final determination on learners' understanding.

Graphic Organizers

Graphic organizers consist of Venn diagrams, word or idea webs, word clouds, concept maps, and other visual representations of knowledge. Learners can complete graphic organizers on paper or on the computer, using technology tools such as Google Drawing. Graphic organizers can be used during a lecture or class reading as a method for learners to take notes or to organize knowledge after a learning activity. Graphic organizers also are a good tool for educators who want to get a sense of what learners view as important and to ensure that learners understand the connections between concepts.

Completion of Authentic Tasks

Learner completion of an authentic learning task can be its own type of formative assessment. An authentic learning task should reflect a real-world application of knowledge and skills, such as writing a picture book, engaging in a debate, creating a Rube Goldberg machine, or making art from trash. Learner performance on the task is evaluated for content knowledge, for learner skills, or for both.

Thumb Survey

If time does not allow for learners to produce something, formative assessment can be accomplished with one-question surveys that ask learners how comfortable they are with the content. For example, in "Imagining: Exploring Scientists," learners examine the idea that anyone can become a scientist. If time does not permit learners to draw two pictures, as suggested in the activity, the instructor may ask learners if they believe they can become a scientist and have them give a thumbs-up for yes, a thumbs-down for no, and a thumbs-sideways for maybe.

• • • • • •

Regardless of how or when assessment is conducted, be sure to review the assessment after the instruction and use the information to better meet the needs of your learners. This enhancement might take the form of content review, the integration of new content, reinforcement of a specific skill in a subsequent lesson, or a revision of the lesson itself for implementation with another group of learners. Also, take advantage of collaboration with other educators and share the results of the learner assessment, even if it's just a general observation of learners' understanding. This sharing will enable your collaborators to help clarify or build upon learners' understanding more effectively during their individual instruction as well as your collaborative lessons.

CONCLUSION
Moving from Inspiration to Collaboration

The hope with this book is that you will be inspired to engage in STEAM practices, a growth mindset, and greater collaboration between school librarians and other educators in the future. Whether you try one activity or all fourteen, consider how STEAM education can be addressed with any grade level in as little as thirty minutes. Don't let lack of time or inspiration stop you before you've begun. Find inspiration here, collaborate with your colleagues, and help your learners see how they can inquire, explore, design, and grow through the exploration of STEAM concepts.

The STEAM approach to the curriculum bridges the gaps between science, technology, mathematics, and art, helping learners to see the connections between each discipline. In this sort of transdisciplinary approach, each subject area is considered as a whole and interconnected idea, rather than as a discrete unit. When learners see the connections between art and science or between mathematics and art, they will be more likely to experience the complexity and depth of each idea.

However, thirty minutes is not enough time to fully grasp the complexity of a topic. Remember that each activity in this book is a starting point, not a destination. Learners will begin to explore and understand each idea, but they will not have time to pursue a complete inquiry unit or to engage fully in an iterative design process. Nevertheless, they can be exposed to these ideas and begin to think with a growth mindset. A growth mindset, combined with proper assessment and reflection, can enable both educator and learner to begin to acknowledge "failures" as learning opportunities and their skills and abilities as a notch in a ladder they can continue to climb.

With effective collaboration, educators can extend the learning opportunities in these thirty-minute activities to enable learners to complete the inquiry process, finish the iterative design process, engage in building more Competencies from the *National School Library Standards*, refine their artistic endeavors, and further explore the transdisciplinary connections presented.

Finally, use the activities presented here as inspiration for writing your own scaffolded lesson plan using the guidance in part 3 of the book. The potential for STEAM learning and collaboration is endless—make sure your learners are a part of it!

Google Sheets Instructions

This appendix supports the use of technology extensions. All explanations given here are specifically for using Google Sheets in a web browser and not in the Google Sheets mobile application. Many explanations will be different in the Google Sheets app on a mobile device. Google Support (http://support.google.com) provides excellent explanations for how to use Google Sheets on a mobile device. Note that all instructions are subject to change because Google periodically releases updates and makes modifications to its services.

MATERIALS REQUIRED AND CLASS SETUP

Google Accounts

For the technology integration explorations, you will need a laptop, desktop, or mobile device with an Internet browser (Safari, Firefox, Chrome) and an educator Google account. If learners will be working on their own sheets, they will also need Google accounts.

Classroom Management with Devices

If you are using a mobile device, such as an iPad, you will need the Google Sheets app. It is highly recommended that learners share a single device in pairs or small groups to help build STEAM collaboration skills. In many of the lessons, it is recommended that the classroom educator manage the Google Sheet and share it on a screen. This is a good opportunity to have different learners manage the computer, such as entering data or creating a graph. If learners will be partnered and using their own copy of the sheet, you may wish to create an anchor chart with guidelines for being a good computer partner (e.g., the driver steers the computer, the navigator provides instructions).

Log-On Tips

For ideas on how to quickly help younger learners log on to Google Apps, see Christine Pinto's website (http://christinepinto.com/).

CREATE A NEW SHEET

1. Log on to Google Drive (http://drive.google.com).
2. Click on New on the left, and choose Google Sheets.

ADDING SHEETS

1. To add a new sheet, click on + in the bottom left of the window.
2. To make a duplicate of a sheet, click on the arrow to the right of the sheet name and choose Duplicate (figure A1).
3. To rename the sheet, click on the arrow next to the name of the new sheet and choose Rename.

FIGURE A1

DUPLICATE SHEET

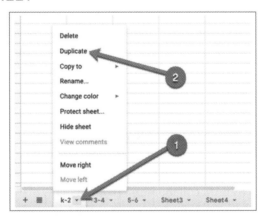

SHARING SHEETS

1. Click on the Share button at the top right.
2. In the new window, click on Get shareable link at the top right. Make sure the sheet is set to View (this is your master copy; you do not want learners to change this). Share this link with your learners.

Tips for Sharing Google Sheets

1. You may wish to use a web address shortener such as Bitly to reduce the size of the URL and make it easier to share with learners. Alternatively, you can put the link on your class web page, learning management system, or the like.

2. Always share a view-only version of your main copy so that learners cannot change your original. If you want learners to be able to make a copy for themselves, edit the URL by changing "edit" at the very end to "copy" before shortening it or sharing it with learners. This revised link will prompt learners to make a copy when they visit the link. Alternatively, when learners open the view-only link, instruct them to click on File and choose Make a Copy.

3. Freezing the header rows prevents learners from changing the titles of columns. To freeze a column or row, click on View > Freeze and select the desired rows or columns.

4. Learners can share their completed sheet with you by sharing it to your e-mail address. If your school or district uses Google Apps for Education, learners may see your e-mail pop up when they type in your name.

FORMATTING TEXT OR CELLS AND MENU OPTIONS

Formatting bar (figure A2, numbered from left to right):

1. Bold: Change text to bold
2. Fill color: Fill cells with color
3. Merge cells: Select more than one cell and click this button to combine them into a single cell
4. Text wrapping: For text that overflows a cell, click this button to wrap it to stay in the cell boundary walls
5. Insert chart (see "Choosing and Setting Up Charts" later in this appendix)

FIGURE A2

FORMATTING BAR

Menu options (figure A3, numbered from left to right):

1. File: Make a Copy, Print, Version History, and so on
2. View: Freeze rows or columns, turn off and on Gridlines, Zoom, and so on
3. Insert: Add images, charts, checkboxes, new sheets, and so on
4. Format: Conditional formatting, and so on
5. Data: Data validation, and so on

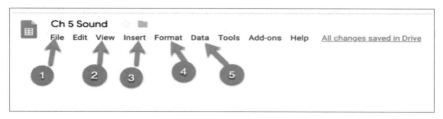

FIGURE A3

MENU OPTIONS

COPYING AND PASTING TEXT

Option 1: Copy/Paste using Menu Ribbon
1. Select the desired cell(s). To do this, click, hold, and drag across all desired cells and then release the mouse button.
2. Click on Edit and then Copy.
3. Click in the first cell that you want to paste into, then click Edit and select Paste.

Option 2: Keyboard Shortcut for Copy/Paste
1. Select the cells you wish to copy (see option 1). On the keyboard, press Command-C (Mac) or Ctrl+C (Windows).
2. Click in the first cell you want to paste to, then press Command-V (Mac) or Ctrl+V (Windows) on keyboard to paste.

Option 3: Right-Click Menu
1. Select the cells you wish to copy (see option 1). If using a two-button mouse, right-click. If using a single-button mouse, hold down the Ctrl button on the keyboard and then click with the mouse. Select Copy or Paste from the menu depending on the action you wish to perform.

FILL COLOR

Fill cells with color.
1. Select the desired cells. Click on the Fill Color button and select the desired color.

AUTOFILL

Autofill allows the contents of one cell to be copied to other cells without having to change or reference each new row. This procedure allows patterns (series) to be created or equations sequenced based on the data in each row.

1. Select the cell that you want to copy the data from.
2. Click the small box in the lower right corner of the selection, and drag down or across to the cells you wish to fill (figure A4).
3. Contents will autofill to the cells. Depending on what you are dragging (text, number, or equation), the contents will copy directly, paste into a pattern, or adjust the equation to reflect each row or column or both.

AUTOFILL

PASTE SPECIAL / TRANSPOSE

Duplicate data by copying and pasting values only, without formatting.
1. Copy the desired content.
2. Click where you wish to paste. Click on the Edit menu and select Paste Special or right-click and select Paste Special (figure A5).

PASTE SPECIAL

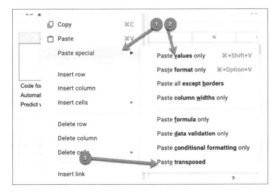

3. Select the desired option:
   a. For pasting values without formatting or equations, select Paste Values Only.
   b. For pasting data transposed, select Paste Transposed.

RESIZING ROWS OR COLUMNS

Change column and row height and width.
1. Select an entire column or row by clicking on the column title (gray lettered or numbered box). To select multiple rows or columns, click and drag. Alternatively, hold down Shift and click on the last row or column you wish to add to select all the rows or columns in between or hold down Command (Mac) or Ctrl (Windows) and select each individual column or row.
2. To resize all the selected rows or columns, place the cursor between two of the header cells until the cursor changes to an arrow, then click and drag to resize.
3. Alternatively, right-click on a row or column header and choose Resize Columns (figure A6).

FIGURE A6

RESIZING COLUMNS

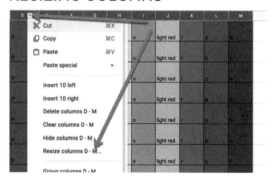

ADD BORDERS

1. Select the desired cells.
2. Click on the Borders button and select the desired options. For solid lines around each cell, select All Borders (figure A7).

FIGURE A7

BORDERS

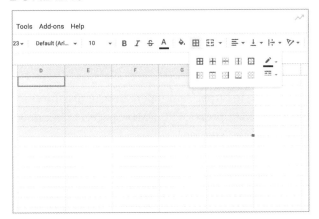

CREATING GRIDS

To create a grid of square boxes, follow the instructions for resizing the desired columns and rows so they are square, then add borders.

INSERT AN IMAGE

Add images into cells for visual ordering.

1. Click on Insert in the Google menu and choose Image. Choose "image in cell" or "image over cells" as desired. Then click on the Search tab. Type in a search term, such as *light bulb,* click on the desired image to select it, and then click the Select button at the bottom of the window (figure A8).

FIGURE A8

INSERT IMAGE

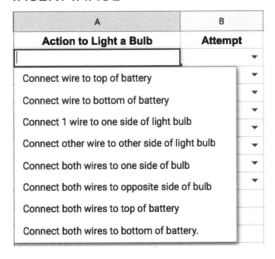

INSERT AN ICON

Add icons into cells to represent data or create rating scales.

1. To insert a star into a cell, type the following equation into the cell: =char(HEX2DEC(2605))
2. To insert the biceps emoji into a cell, type the following equation into the cell: =CHAR(HEX2DEC("1F4AA"))

To find more emoji and symbol codes, go to https://emojipedia.org or use the emoji finder on your computer keyboard. On a Mac, press CTRL-CMD-Space. For Windows, press Windows+; (semicolon) or Windows+. (period).

INSERT A CHECKBOX

Add a checkbox to a single cell or several cells.

1. Select the cells that will have checkboxes.
2. Click on the Insert menu and select Checkbox.

CREATING A FORM

Forms allow you to collect data from users and then place their responses into a spreadsheet (figure A9).

FIGURE A9

FORM

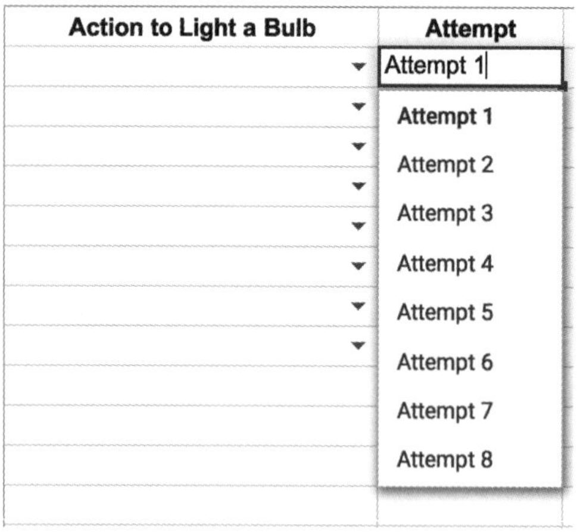

Action to Light a Bulb	Attempt
▾	Attempt 1
▾	Attempt 1
▾	Attempt 2
▾	Attempt 3
▾	Attempt 4
▾	Attempt 5
▾	Attempt 6
	Attempt 7
	Attempt 8

1. Log on to Google Drive, click the + New button and then More to choose Google Forms.
2. Choose the question type: Multiple choice, Short answer, and the like.

3. Add another question.
4. View the live form to collect responses.
5. View the responses and send to a Google Sheet.

PRINTING

Allows spreadsheets to be printed.
1. To print the entire sheet, click the Print button or the File menu and then Print.
2. To print a specific set of cells, select all cells that you want to print first and then click the Print button or File > Print.
3. Click the print drop-down menu and select either Current sheet or Selected cells.
4. Click Next and then Print.

EQUATIONS

Equations allow for mathematical calculations in cells. They can also be used with conditional formatting to create automatic formatting (see "Conditional Formatting").
1. Type the equals sign (=) in the cell.
2. Type the rest of the equation. Use "+" to add, "-" to subtract, "*" to multiply, and "/" to divide, or use commands such as SUM to complete a particular action. For example, =SUM(C1:C4) will add together the values of cells C1, C2, C3, and C4 (figure A10).
3. To repeat the equation in each row, select the cells where the equation was typed and then use Autofill to copy the equation to other cells (see "Autofill").

FIGURE A10

EQUATION EXAMPLE

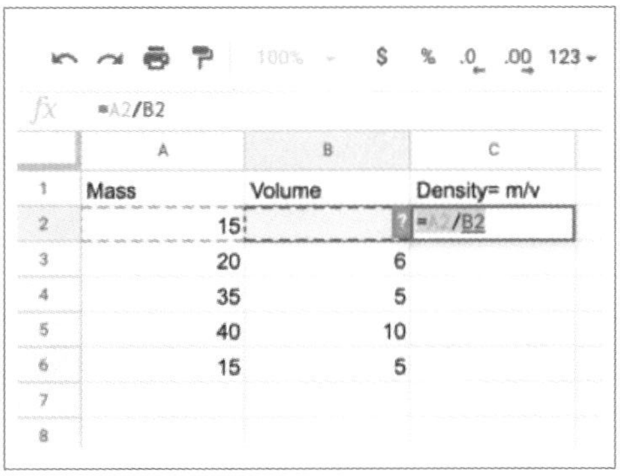

LISTS VIA DATA VALIDATION

Lists are a drop-down menu of items within a cell that a user can select from to fill the cell.

To create a list:

1. Select the cells that will have the List.
2. From the Data menu, choose Data validation (figure A11).

FIGURE A11

DATA VALIDATION

3. In the Data validation window, make sure the Cell range is correct (figure A12, step 1). In the Criteria menu, select "List of items" (see figure A12, step 2) and then enter the list of items to the right separated by commas (see figure A12, step 3).

FIGURE A12

DATA VALIDATION 2

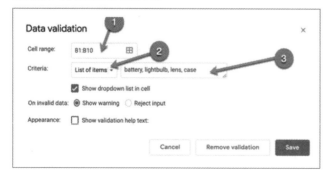

4. Click Save.

CONDITIONAL FORMATTING

1. Select the cells that you wish to format. Click on the Format menu and choose Conditional formatting (figure A13).

CONDITIONAL FORMATTING

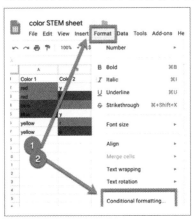

2. In the Conditional format rules window, click on "Single color." The Apply to range should match the selected cells (figure A14, step 1).
3. In the Format cells of the drop-down menu, choose the appropriate option. To have certain words or letters represent specific colors, choose "Text is exactly" (see figure A14, step 2).
4. In the Value or formula box, enter a letter or word to represent a color. For example, type "r" for red (see figure A14, step 3).
5. Click on the Fill Color button in the Formatting style options and choose the corresponding color—red in this example (see figure A14, step 4).
6. Click on + Add another rule at the bottom of the menu and repeat for other colors (see figure A14, step 5). In "Making Dye: Examining Color," the following are recommended: r (red), b (blue), y (yellow), g (green), o (orange), w (white), bl (black), lb (light blue), db (dark blue), lr (light red), dr (dark red), ly (light yellow), dy (dark yellow).
7. When all colors are added, click Done.

FIGURE A14

CONDITIONAL FORMAT RULES

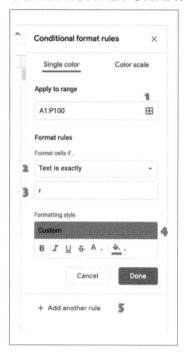

EXPLORE BUTTON

The Explore button suggests charts that may help to visualize data.
1. Select the data you want to include in a chart.
2. Click the star in the lower right-hand corner of the screen (figure A15).

FIGURE A15

EXPLORE BUTTON

3. Choose a chart that best fits your data and purpose (figure A16).

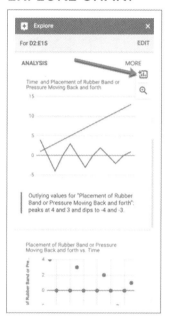

EXPLORE CHART

4. Click the + sign to add the chart to your sheet.

CHOOSING AND SETTING UP CHARTS

When choosing a chart for your data, start by selecting the data that you want to have graphed. Then click the Insert Chart button. When the Chart editor opens to the right, a new chart image appears on the spreadsheet, and you can select a variety of charts from the Chart type drop-down menu. The chart image will change based on the chart type you select. In addition, the chart options for formatting the chart will change based on the chart type chosen. The main options to adjust include the following:

- X-axis: Data on the horizontal axis allow you to change which data are used in the chart, to remove data, or to label the axis.
- Series: Allows you to add labels or notes.
- Switch rows / columns: Turns data in each row into column data.
- Use row 2 as header: Allows you to use the second row as the header title, if it was selected when initial data were selected.

Some technology integration explorations will ask learners to choose a chart to best fit data. The following are general descriptions of when it is best to use each chart type:

- Line chart: Find trends or changes over time (e.g., change in temperature over a month).

- Column chart: Show differences between data; use with Checkboxes (e.g., number of red cars to blue cars).
- Organizational chart: Show relationships between data (e.g., organization of family members).
- Bubble chart: Show effects of one variable on another, with the size of the bubble being the third column data, typically an aggregate (e.g., number and color type of crayons in different crayon boxes).
- Radar chart: Compare three or more sets of data in a radial pattern, in which each variable is a spoke (e.g., budget expenses).

RADAR CHART

1. Select one or more columns of data and then click the Insert Chart button (figure A17, step 1).
2. Select Radar chart from the Chart type menu (see figure A17, step 2).
3. Make sure Data range matches the intended X-axis of the chart (see figure A17, step 3 and step 4).
4. Choose Aggregate column A (see figure A17, step 5).

FIGURE A17

RADAR CHART

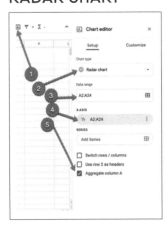

ORGANIZATIONAL CHART

1. Select two columns of data.
2. Click the Insert Chart button.
3. Select Organizational chart from the Chart type menu (figure A18).
4. Make sure "ID" is the first column and "Parent" is the second column.

FIGURE A18

ORGANIZATIONAL CHART

COLUMN CHART OR BAR CHART

1. Select one or two columns of data.
2. Click the Insert Chart button.
3. Select Column chart from the Chart type menu (figure A19).
4. If counting checkboxes or numbers of list items, select "Aggregate column."

FIGURE A19

BAR CHART

LINE CHART

1. Select two columns of data.
2. Click the Insert Chart button.
3. Select Line chart in the Chart type menu (figure A20).
4. Make sure X-axis shows the intended data.
5. If you selected the header row, check "Use row 1 as headers."
6. Check "Use column X as labels."

LINE CHART

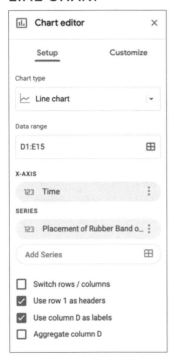

BUBBLE CHART

1. Select three or four columns of data.
2. Click the Insert Chart button.
3. Select Bubble chart from the Chart type menu (figure A21).
4. Change the X-axis, Y-axis, and Series so they reflect the intended data by clicking on three dots to the right of each and choosing Edit.
5. For size, you can choose the column that will best show aggregate data. For example, in "Melted Crayons: States of Matter," temperature could be used.

FIGURE A21

BUBBLE CHART

ELEMENT LOCATION CHART

This chart can be used to locate the activities in which a specific Google Sheet element is used.

GOOGLE SHEETS ELEMENT	Imagining: Exploring Scientists	Making a Tissue Box Guitar: Exploring Sound	Making Dye: Examining Color	Making a Spiderweb: Insect Exploration	Fast Surfaces: Experimenting with Friction	Melted Crayons: States of Matter	String Art: Exploring Patterns	Working Together: Build-a-Tower Challenge	Building a Flashlight: Looking at Circuits	Building a Rube Goldberg Machine: Engineering Challenge	Designing a Thermos: Exploring Heat	Ready to Recycle: Trash-to-Treasure Challenge	Bobbing Boats: Floating and Sinking	Coding with Cups: Designing a Structure Using Code
Sharing Sheets												X		
Fill Color				X										
Autofill							X			X		X		X
Paste Special / Transpose							X							
Creating Grids			X				X							
Insert an Image	X			X	X				X					X
Insert an Icon								X						
Insert a Checkbox		X						X	X					
Creating a Form	X													
Printing				X										
Equations				X		X	X					X		
Lists via Data Validation				X					X	X				
Conditional Formatting			X				X							
Explore Button				X					X	X			X	
Choosing and Setting Up Charts											X	X		
Radar Chart	X													
Organizational Chart		X								X				
Column Chart or Bar Chart		X			X					X				
Line Chart		X		X	X	X						X	X	X
Bubble Chart						X								

BIBLIOGRAPHY

AASL American Association of School Librarians. 2018. *National School Library Standards for Learners, School Librarians, and School Libraries*. Chicago, IL: ALA Editions.

Abrams, L. C., R. Cross, E. Lesser, and D. Z. Levin. 2003. "Nurturing Interpersonal Trust in Knowledge-Sharing Networks." *Academy of Management Executive* 17 (4): 64–77.

Bryk, A. S., and B. Schneider. 2003. "Trust in Schools: A Core Resource for School Reform." *Educational Leadership* 60 (6): 40–45.

Carlson, M. O., G. E. Humphrey, and K. S. Reinhardt. 2003. *Weaving Science Inquiry and Continuous Assessment: Using Formative Assessment to Improve Learning*. Thousand Oaks, CA: Corwin Press.

Catterall, J. S., S. A. Dumais, and G. Hampden-Thompson. 2012. *The Arts and Achievement in At-Risk Youth: Findings from Four Longitudinal Studies*. Washington, DC: National Endowment for the Arts.

Cooper, O., and M. Bray. 2011. "School Library Media Specialist-Teacher Collaboration: Characteristics, Challenges, Opportunities." *TechTrends: Linking Research and Practice to Improve Learning* 55 (4): 48–55.

Cross, R. L., and A. Parker. 2004. *The Hidden Power of Social Networks: Understanding How Work Really Gets Done in Organizations*. Boston, MA: Harvard Business School Press.

Dweck, C. S. 2016. *Mindset: The New Psychology of Success*. New York, NY: Random House.

Eisner, E. 2002. "What the Arts Do for the Young." *School Arts*, 16–17.

Goddard, Y. L., R. D. Goddard, and M. Tschannen-Moran. 2007. "A Theoretical and Empirical Investigation of Teacher Collaboration for School Improvement and Student Achievement in Public Elementary Schools." *Teachers College Record* 109 (4): 877–96.

Good, C., J. Aronson, and M. Inzlicht. 2003. "Improving Adolescents' Standardized Test Performance: An Intervention to Reduce the Effects of Stereotype Threat." *Journal of Applied Developmental Psychology* 24 (6): 645–62. https://doi.org/10.1016/j.appdev.2003.09.002

Graham, N., and L. Brouillette. 2016. "Using Arts Integration to Make Science Learning Memorable in the Upper Elementary Grades: A Quasi-Experimental Study." *Journal for Learning Through the Arts* 12 (1).

Hetland, L., and E. Winner. 2004. "Cognitive Transfer from Arts Education to Nonarts Outcomes: Research Evidence and Policy Implications." In *Handbook of Research and Policy in Arts Education,* edited by E. W. Eisner and M. D. Day, 135–61. Mahwah, NJ: Lawrence Erlbaum Associates.

Inholder, I., and J. Piaget. 1958. *The Growth of Logical Thinking from Childhood to Adolescence.* New York, NY: Routledge.

Jauk, E., Benedek, M., and A. C. Neubauer. 2012. "Tackling Creativity at Its Roots: Evidence for Different Patterns of EEG Alpha Activity Related to Convergent and Divergent Modes of Task Processing." *International Journal of Psychophysiology* 84 (2): 219–25. https://doi.org/10.1016/j.ijpsycho.2012.02.012

Leana, C. R., and F. K. Pil. 2006. "Social Capital and Organizational Performance: Evidence from Urban Public Schools." *Organization Science* 17 (3): 353–66.

Limb, C. J., and A. R. Braun. 2008. "Neural Substrates of Spontaneous Musical Performance: An fMRI Study of Jazz Improvisation." *PLoS ONE* 3 (2): e1679.

Lottero-Perdue, P. S., and E. A. Parry. 2017. "Perspectives on Failure in the Classroom by Elementary Teachers New to Teaching Engineering." *Journal of Pre-College Engineering Education Research* 7 (1): 47–67. https://doi.org/10.7771/2157-9288.1158.

National Research Council. 2012. *A Framework for K–12 Science Education: Practices, Crosscutting Concepts, and Core Ideas.* Washington, DC: National Academies Press. https://doi.org/10.17226/13165.

———. 2013. *Next Generation Science Standards: For States, By States.* Washington, DC: National Academies Press. https://doi.org/10.17226/18290.

O'Brien, M., J. Fielding-Wells, K. Makar, and J. Hillman. 2015. "How Inquiry Pedagogy Enables Teachers to Facilitate Growth Mindsets in Mathematics Classrooms." *Proceedings of the 38th Annual Conference of the Mathematics Education Research Group of Australasia*, 469–76. Sunshine Coast, Queensland, Australia: Mathematics Education Research Group of Australasia.

OECD. 2014. A *Teachers' Guide to TALIS 2013: Teaching and Learning International Survey.* TALIS, OECD Publishing. Retrieved from https://www.oecd.org/edu/school/TALIS-Teachers-Guide.pdf.

Rinne, L., E. Gregory, J. Yarmolinskaya, and M. Hardiman. 2011. "Why Arts Integration Improves Long-Term Retention of Content." *Mind, Brain, and Education* 5 (2): 89–96. https://doi.org/10.1111/j.1751-228X.2011.01114.x.

Ronfeldt, M., S. O. Farmer, K. McQueen, and J. A. Grissom. 2015. "Teacher Collaboration in Instructional Teams and Student Achievement." *American Educational Research Journal* 52 (3): 475–514. https://doi.org/10.3102/0002831215585562.

SEADAE State Education Agencies Directors of Arts Education. 2015. *National Core Arts Standards.*

Smith, T., R. Brumskill, A. Johnson, and T. Zimmer. 2018. "The Impact of Teacher Language on Students' Mindsets and Statistics Performance." *International Journal* 21 (4): 775–86. https://doi.org/10.1007/s11218-018-9444-z.

Sousa, D. A., and T. Pilecki. 2012. *From STEM to STEAM: Using Brain-Compatible Strategies to Integrate the Arts*. Thousand Oaks, CA: Corwin Press.

———, and C. A. Tomlinson. 2011. *Differentiation and the Brain: How Neuroscience Supports the Learner-Friendly Classroom*. Bloomington, IN: Solution Tree Press.

Takeuchi, H., Y. Taki, Y. Sassa, H. Hashizume, A. Sekiguchi, A. Fukushima, and R. Kawashima. 2010. "White Matter Structures Associated with Creativity: Evidence from Diffusion Tensor Imaging." *NeuroImage* 51 (1): 11–18. https://doi.org/10.1016/j.neuroimage.2010.02.035

Yager, R. E. 2007. "STS Requires Changes in Teaching." *Bulletin of Science, Technology and Society* 27 (5): 386–90. https://doi.org/10.1177/0270467607305737.

CONTRIBUTOR

Christina Hum, MEd Technology, is a science educator in Fairbanks, Alaska. She is currently developing and teaching online science and mathematics courses for at-risk learners in Alaska. She has worked as an educational technology coach and online specialist for Fairbanks the North Star Borough School District. In addition, she was a videoconference content provider in her business, providing asynchronous and synchronous Alaska-based content and projects for learners around the world. She has developed and implemented curriculum in media literacy for the Alaska Injury Prevention Center, learner leadership for the ReInventing Schools Coalition, and science summer camps for Denali National Park. She is the author of *The Straight Cliff 300: An Educational Dog Racing Adventure.*

INDEX